Elephants & Tappers

MICHAEL THORP, AISP

Marshall Cavendish

Copyright © 2009 Marshall Cavendish International (Asia) Private Limited

Cover design: Lock Hong Liang
Cover images: Goran Anicic, Benedeki (sxc.hu) and Vicky S

Published by Marshall Cavendish Editions
An imprint of Marshall Cavendish International
1 New Industrial Road, Singapore 536196

Other Marshall Cavendish Offices
Marshall Cavendish Ltd. 5th Floor, 32–38 Saffron Hill, London EC1N 8FH, UK • Marshall Cavendish Corporation. 99 White Plains Road, Tarrytown NY 10591-9001, USA • Marshall Cavendish International (Thailand) Co Ltd. 253 Asoke, 12th Flr, Sukhumvit 21 Road, Klongtoey Nua, Wattana, Bangkok 10110, Thailand • Marshall Cavendish (Malaysia) Sdn Bhd, Times Subang, Lot 46, Subang Hi-Tech Industrial Park, Batu Tiga, 40000 Shah Alam, Selangor Darul Ehsan, Malaysia

Marshall Cavendish is a trademark of Times Publishing Limited

National Library Board Singapore Cataloguing in Publication Data

Thorp, Michael, 1936-
Elephants, tigers and tappers : recollections of a British rubber planter in Malaya / Michael Thorp. Singapore : Marshall Cavendish Travel, 2008.
p. cm.
ISBN-13 : 978-981-261-746-0
ISBN-10 : 981-261-746-9

1. Thorp, Michael, 1936- 2. Rubber plantation workers – Malaysia – Malaya – Biography. 3. Plantation life – Malaysia – Malaya – History. 4. English – Malaysia – Malaya – Biography. I. Title.

HD8039.R92
633.8952092 -- dc22   OCN258850915

Printed in Singapore by Times Graphics Pte Ltd

Contents

CHAPTER 1

Do You Play Cricket?

I was part of the madness of the Empire. It was a madness that paved the way for a British, London-based rubber company to employ a bumptious, twenty-year-old boy with no real life experience and send him on a journey to Malaya, to become a Rubber Planter. It was part of the colonial madness that reached back to a gun-runner, Francis Light, who visited the Malay coast in 1770. He discovered that Dutch influence did not stretch as far north as Kedah and that Siamese influence did not stretch as far south, so he urged the East India Company to found a settlement in the area. That, however, was not part of the Companyís policy, the directors already having a far larger empire than they knew what to do with. Light might have implored forever in vain, had not the War of American Independence (1775–83) come to alter the whole situation.

I was first employed as an Assistant Planter in a dismal London office in 1956, at the age of twenty. I was three years older than Sir Hugh Clifford, another huge figure who helped cement British interests in Malaya. In 1883, he was only seventeen when he was first employed in the Colonial Service. He went on to be Governor of the Straits Settlements. When I started planting, I probably had only a third of Sir Hugh's intelligence and nothing like his dedication. The reason I mention Hugh Clifford is because he and I, in some small measure, share a complicated and absorbing involvement with the State of Pahang—but more of that later.

Frankly, when I signed up to go to Malaya I had no idea of what I was going to. My father had to witness my signature and sign the contract because I had not, at the time of employment, achieved my majority, as reaching the age of twenty-one was so grandly termed. My father also had to sign on my behalf when I went to sea as an indentured apprentice. On both occasions, aware of the implications for him as a parent with the possibility of recrimination at some later date, he cautioned me before he signed: "Is this really what you want to do?"

"Yes it is Dad." I answered impatiently, slightly irritated that he should choose to show fatherly concern at this somewhat late stage.

I knew nothing about planting. My knowledge of botany was only rudimentary school botany and biology. The company I was to work for gave no training, no briefing, not even a simple training course to introduce me to the complicated ethnic structure of Malaya. All I knew before I set out for my new country was just what I could pick up in the reference section of the Reigate Public Library.

However, I did write a letter to my brother who was serving in the British Royal Air Force in Kuala Lumpur at the time. As far as I could understand he was servicing combat helicopters and himself undergoing jungle survival courses. He wrote back, and, in no uncertain terms, told me that because of the state of emergency in the country Planters were being shot all over the place, and on no account was I to consider such employment. Young men are stupid and full of ideas of their own immunity from pain, discomfort and unpleasantness. At the age of twenty it seems that adventure beckoned with an irresistible force.

In October 1956 I was called in for an interview in the London offices of The Pahang Consolidated Company Limited, a tin mining company in Malaya and the parent company of The Kuala Reman Rubber Estates Ltd. Mr Gordon Fairmaid, a bespectacled New Zealander with a surprisingly boyish crew cut, was Chairman of the Company. He had previously been General Manager of the tin mine at Sungai Lembing, some 40 kilometres due west of Kuantan. As a mining engineer who had worked his way up to become General Manager in Malaya and then Chairman of The Board of Directors in London, he had years of service with the company, and I was in total awe of a man who had obviously spent his whole life in the East. At that interview I remember Fairmaid as a surprisingly mild and gentle person who obviously had years of experience from Malaya, but was considerate enough to answer the most naïve questions. Subsequently, and with hindsight I suspect his affability was directed at the need to recruit a feisty young man, indeed, any young man, rather than reveal the more steely side of his nature.

"I see from your CV that you were an apprentice in the Merchant Navy, and you've had experience with Kroo labour on vessels sailing up and down the West Coast of Africa." He looked over the top of his glasses. "What is an apprentice?"

"It's like a cadet, Sir. A junior officer, but with indentures to stay with the same company for your sea time."

"I see from your letter you have had an accident to your shoulder. Is that all cleared up?"

"Yes, Sir," I replied, dishonestly rubbing the wound still suppurating from unabsorbed internal stitches.

"You don't want to go back to sea then?" Again he peered at me over the top of his spectacles to examine my face and catch any fleeting trace of emotion or feeling that my answer would bring. I had prepared a reply for exactly this moment, and decided that now was the time to trot it out.

"While I have been recovering from the surgery to my shoulder I have been working in my company's shipping offices in Plantation House, in Fenchurch Street. The building is full of rubber companies and the Commodity Exchange is on the ground floor. I have found it all very interesting, I have asked questions during my lunch hour and I've spoken to quite a number of people about the plantation industry. When I saw your advertisement in the Daily Telegraph, things just seemed to fall into place."

I did not want to explain that from my almost three years at sea, I had discovered that a career as a mariner was not what I wanted for the rest of my life.

I loved the sea, the immensity of the ocean and the endless skies. And I really missed the exhilaration of being on a ship in heavy weather. Those deliciously fearful and exciting moments of living on the edge, intense feelings of fear and delight when hanging on to the wing of the bridge watching the foredeck punch into head seas and the feel the shudder and whoosh as the bow slammed water in a hissing spray out past the sides of the ship to be whipped away by the wind. That fear, that exhilaration, sharpened my youthful appreciation of being alive; and that, that humming in my body, I loved. But the make and break of leaving home and living in such confined quarters, of having to share months at sea with people with whom I had nothing in common, put me off the seaman's life.

Perhaps the real trouble was, that I had no idea what I wanted to do with my life. Unlike some of my friends who, at the age of sixteen or so, declared that they wanted to be chemists, or journalists or study medicine, I really had no idea of which way to go or what direction to take. All I really knew was that I felt an overwhelming sense of living in a world that somehow offered more than my own home town of Reigate could offer; more than the drudgery of travelling on a crowded and uncomfortable train to London every morning and then, after a day's work checking accounts, facing up to the reverse journey home again late in the evening. My senses told me that the world was enormous, full of challenge and adventure. I wanted to experience as much of it as I could.

Mr Fairmaid seemed satisfied with my answer.

"Do you play cricket?" he demanded.

"Yes, I do, Sir." I replied. "My batting needs some work but I am opening fast bowler for my team." I failed to mention that my team was The Panther pub from Doods Road in Reigate, and if anyone could get their arm over with a cricket ball they more or less qualified as an opening bowler.

"Good," Mr Fairmaid said, "Take your bat then." He smiled and stood up and extended his hand, and I knew I had got the job.

"George Watson, the Company Secretary will talk to you about the details of travel, and salary and what not. When can you leave?"

"I have to give a month's notice, Sir."

"Well, you'd better do that right away."

George Watson was a dry little man with copious amounts of brilliantine slicking down his hair that looked as if it had been painted on. Glossy black, the brush strokes of hair stopped short of his excessively wrinkled forehead and gave him a constantly anxious and serious look.

"Well you see, Mr Thorp," he explained, "in Malaya we do not refer to a plantation as such, it is usually called an estate." He continued filling in the form on the desk in front of him as he examined my certificate of birth. "Although an estate is of course a plantation, rather large, some of them are thousands of acres." He noted down school results and the names of references. "At Kuala Reman Rubber Estates," he continued, "We have about 4,500 acres of planted rubber, split into three separate divisions, or estates." He busied himself in noting down further details and handed me back all my papers. "Technically, Mr Thorp, you will require the signature of your father or next of kin when it comes to sign the contract." He folded his hands in front of him as if in prayer. "You see, you are not 21 until July next year, and this is October and we shall want you to leave for Malaya, for the estate that is, as soon as possible."

I asked George Watson for more information about the job and what sort of tasks would be expected of me.

"The title of Rubber Planter is something of a misnomer," he began earnestly, at the same time inviting me to make notes. "The Planter, does not actually go around the estate and plant rubber trees. He is the company's representative who manages the running of the whole estate. He is in some ways much more than a Managing Director as he has responsibility for the welfare and well-being of the labour force. On Kuala Reman, altogether we employ about 650 people and we have our own housing for about 2,500 people, including dependants. We have our own medical arrangements, each division has its own qualified hospital dresser and the doctor from Sungai Lembing, from the tin mine, the parent company in fact, visits all three divisions once a month."

A very elderly lady appeared with tea and a tin of Huntley & Palmer biscuits. George Watson made a point of waiting for her to put everything in its correct place, and then displayed overdone courtesy by thanking her several times to her obvious embarrassment. "We don't have the heart to sack her," he explained. "Edith has been our tea lady for more years than I can remember."

"Now, to get back to your duties; you will join Mr Cotterill, who is the Manager. He will tell you what to do and explain how things work, and your job will be to fulfill the duties of assistant, his assistant manager." We both drank our tea. "Mind you, if I may offer a word of advice."

"Oh, please do," I said, far too eagerly.

"If I were you, I would make it my business to find out as much about planting as possible from Mr Cotterill, as he will be retiring in about a year's time. And, of course, I would make it my business to find out as much as possible about the job: the production of rubber in the factory, tapping, drainage, terracing and surveying, accounting and book-keeping; you know, all the things that a Planter needs to know."

When I was back out on the streets of London, on London Wall, I thought I would explode with uncontainable excitement. It was like having a rocket straight up through my body and if someone had ignited the touch paper I would have roared off in the direction of my beloved stars. I was twenty, and I had my life and the world ahead of me.

Mother, of course, was not so pleased. "Don't know why you can't just settle down here in the job you already have in London. You have a nice girlfriend, why throw it all away? Stay here!" She worked busily at the kitchen sink with the washing up. With a smoker's grimace, a Kensitas fag dangled from the corner of her mouth. Our serious conversations always took place over the washing up. "Time to think," she used to say, "To take stock." I continued to explain what a wonderful opportunity it was for me. And furthermore, Pahang, at least the part of the State in which I would be working, was a declared "White Area", that is to say, that there were no longer any Communist Terrorists operating in the area.

"I think you should stay here." She said, the back of her wet hand came up to her forehead to push a strand of hair out of her eyes, a familiar move that the whole family knew was caused by smoke. "Much safer here." The last saucepan finished, she doused her cigarette out in the washing-up water. "I can't understand it.

Why you have to go traipsing off to Malaya." I recognised the signs, the puckering of the lips and the trembling of her chin. My mother was crying.

"Come on Mum," I said, putting my arms around her. "I'll be fine."

"You are the second of our sons to go out to that place, and sometimes I can't get to sleep at night wondering what's happening to Jim. There he is, fighting in the jungle, with ambushes." She sniffed and quickly recovered, dabbing her eyes with her apron. "Well, Jim is coming home now," she said, looking at me through her tears. "So, just when I thought I could relax, you have to go traipsing off out there." I could hear the pain in her voice, but there is an odd capacity in young men who are on the point of breaking away from home to brush the hurt and pain they cause aside. All things are subsidiary, even mothers, to the excitement of a challenging and different future.

Magnificent snake

I have seen some snakes. I have certainly had a few close calls. I have almost stepped on snakes. I have had them intertwined in coitus by my head and shoulders when I leaned my chair back to rest on a notice board. But I have never in my whole life in the East been so terrified and amazed as that morning in the Mini-Moke.

I was Acting Manager on Jabor Valley Estate while the Manager John Dickie was on leave in Scotland. I had been to the southern part of the estate to check on the collection of latex at a weighing station in Field 5. The station was just a shed, a weighing station, where tappers carried their latex and scrap. The latex was tested for dry rubber content and poured into a large aluminium bucket, which was weighed. The number of pounds was entered in the field books before the tractor towed the tank to the factory.

It was the hottest part of the day, approaching 2:00 pm. The sun was like a smiting hand that had temporarily beaten the world into burning silence. I decided to take a short cut on my way back to the bungalow for lunch. The road took me along the edge of our estate and through a few acres of smallholding, an unkempt stand of old rubber submerged in Straits rhododendron, Siam weed and lalang. The Mini-Moke was fun to drive, as it was low to the ground with no doors, something like an over-sized Go-Kart.

I was driving slowly because of the poor state of the road. Suddenly, moving from right to left and only fifteen paces in front of the bonnet there was an olive green snake, its head and first few feet of its body well above the ground, above the level of my eyes. The only word I can find to describe what happened is to say that he whooshed across the road and into the lallang. I watched the lalang be laid over, first to one side then to the other. Whoosh, whoosh. The snake was moving so fast that within just a few seconds all that was left to tell that it had been there at all, were the still moving shrubs in the path of its passage. The field road at that point was at least ten feet wide, and he had stretched across the whole width of the road. I do not exaggerate when I say he was as thick as my lower leg. He was a magnificent snake indeed, he was a king, a king cobra.

C.J. Windsor told me once that a mature king cobra is able to move as fast as a galloping horse. I didn't pay much attention at the time. But I can assure you it is true. The speed of that snake moving across the road and into the lalang was stupefying. It left me with great respect for that particular snake and also left me feeling apprehensive should I ever come face to face with one when walking, with only my stick to protect me. But, I calmed myself with the thought that a serpent that had lived to be that size must be skilful at staying away from harm. Such a snake would avoid contact with man as surely as we would prefer to have no close encounter with the snake.

CHAPTER 2

The Voyage Out, On The *Willem Ruys*

Between Christmas, 1956 and the new year of 1957, my sister and brother-in-law drove me from my hometown of Reigate, in Surrey to the ship. They spent half an hour looking around the elegant *Willem Ruys*, where I was booked in as a second-class passenger. They walked ashore just before she sailed. and waved me farewell from a rain-soaked Southampton as the great, black-hulled, Dutch ship moved out with a tug escort down the darkening Solent towards the Isle of Wight and the open sea. We were set to sail around Africa via Cape Town rather than through the Suez Canal. The Canal was still littered with sunken vessels and the French and British were busily engaged in trying to keep possession of Egyptian territory. I shared a cabin with a Methodist minister on his way to North Borneo. I remember him as a kindly man who was sparing with his advice, and, although he must have been in his forties, he treated me like an adult. I liked him for that.

It was wonderful to be back at sea again but this time as a passenger. As the lights of the Solent rapidly disappeared, I distinctly recall dropping a piece of wrapping paper on deck. Youthfully appalled at my own thoughtlessness, I turned back and retrieved it. I remember thinking to myself as I picked it up again; that ingrained goodness, a sense of fair play, honesty and integrity would be required of me. And I was ready. I dropped the crushed paper into a wastebasket with a satisfying sense of virtue and having played the game.

"Aren't you a good boy," exclaimed a woman who was well wrapped up in an expensive fur coat. She had crutches under her arms as one of her legs was encased in a plaster cast.

"Here, help me get something from my bag." When I moved closer to her I could see that she was a very attractive woman. A lovely blond, mid-thirties, perhaps even older, carefully made up with a slightly smallish and somewhat spiteful mouth. We shook hands. Her name was Anne.

"Just hold these damn crutches," she said in an exasperated manner, "they are guaranteed to fall down if I lean them up against something." She fished a packet of cigarettes out of her bag and offered me one. I lit her cigarette, then my own in the same suave, smouldering way that I had watched Cary Grant perform in the movies.

Much later in the voyage, in another scene, which could also have come right out of the movies, I kissed her. It was a starlit night on the deck of an ocean liner that was gently ploughing its way through a tropical velvet sea, and I was young with the fervour that burns inside a twenty-year-old. The ocean hissed by and the unfamiliar stars dipped as the ship rolled gently on the Indian Ocean.

A couple of days later, Anne invited me into to her single-berth cabin to wash her hair. This I did. I washed her hair. I washed her hair! I did not attempt to kiss her although I think she was expecting me to, and I left it at that. The Boy Scout good conduct code made me repeat to myself that I had a girlfriend at home in Reigate, well, she was in Horley. Good Boy Scouts do not play fast and loose with beautiful women on ocean liners on the very first opportunity that presents itself. And, although I was on the Dutch flagship sailing off to spend four years away from her (my contract contained a clause forbidding marriage during the first four year term of employment) I felt it behove me to be true to my love, and those honest principles of my growing up.

Honestly! I have kicked myself for that many times since. But who knows how life is going to turn out, when you are twenty and locked in a cabin on a wonderful ocean liner with an incredibly gorgeous woman? If Anne is still alive I take my hat off to her, and thank her for her understanding. She allowed me to walk out of her cabin, softly closing the door, with a priggish feeling of virtue. I said 'no' for the Empire. How proud my housemaster, Mr Coupland, and the other exponents of cold showers of my youth would have been.

Travelling with me and the 600 or so other passengers on the *Willem Ruys* was a British Wing Commander. Like me, he was in second class, together with his wife and two young children. It was said that he discovered that there were other British officers of junior rank travelling first class. After the vessel had called in at Cape Town and sailed off in the direction of Ceylon, when we were somewhere off Madagascar, we were kept busy for the best part of a day by muster drills, fire drills and stand-by-your-bunk drills. Frequently we heard increasingly ominous announcements over the loud speaker, "Would Wing Commander so and so please report to the purser on B deck." Somewhat later in the day, as the level of rumour increased, the general mood of the passengers became more and more despondent. The final announcement was broadcast over the loudspeaker system about six in the evening. It was spoken in the clipped, Dutch accent of the Master.

"Vi are sorry, lidies and chentlemen to ennounce that Ving Commander so and so is missing. If anyvun hes seen him, or thinks they hev seen him please contact the perser immejiately. Because of se time elapsed since we first received se report that he was missing there is no point in turning back to search for him in the ocean. Ve vill not be having any dancing diss evening as mark of respect."

He jumped! He left his wife and the two children and he jumped overboard. Rumours then flowed around the ship, amplified by extra rounds of gin and tonic and Scotch and soda. At that time I did not touch alcohol but I consumed a lot of Coca-Cola so I spent time in the bar listening. Variously he was reported as having been seen on the boat deck, hiding in a lifeboat. Apparently someone had heard that his wife and children had gone to breakfast that morning, leaving him in the cabin to follow. It was said that he laid out all the family's documents, passports, tickets, money and travellers-cheques on his neatly made up bunk. There was no mention of a letter to his wife, although, poor woman, a letter may have helped her understand what drove him to it.

We anchored in the harbour in Colombo. A launch came alongside to a service port in the side of the vessel. Most of the passengers lined the decks and silently watched as the wretched woman and her two children were taken ashore.

Now, at this time of my life, I rarely think about this incident. When I was younger I used to tell the story quite frequently, emphasising the thoughtlessness of the man, the selfishness, the callous hurt he inflicted on his wife and children. It was one of the stories I would use in a bar or with a group of people where it is expected that one says something. But as I grow older the story has fallen out of my conversation. Possibly, because I no longer meet so many people. But I hope it is because I have developed enough empathy in life to have reached the stage where I am at last able to hold back on the rapid black and white judgements of youth.

Colombo was a shock. It was my first taste of a busy city on the Indian sub-continent. I was fascinated by the bustle, by the number of people seemingly moving in all directions.

I was intoxicated by the colours, the wonderful ragged palms, the flowers, and the smells. Some of the passengers were taken on an excursion for tea and drinks to the very prestigious Mount Lavinia Hotel. It was here on the terrace, looking out West towards the setting sun that I saw for the first time, the green flash. I had no idea what it was. I thought my eyes were playing tricks on me, so I dismissed it as a result of too much sun, or too much noise, or excitement. I filed the experience away until many years later I read an article in the Readers' Digest, explaining the phenomenon. I then started looking for the flash and, so far, have four to my credit. You need the tropics, a clear horizon and a setting sun. Just as the final limb, the final thinnest of thin parts of the sun's surface drops below the horizon—you may, if God so wishes, and conditions are just right, see an unmistakably brilliant green flash, like a bubble of promise. I think of it, in the same way that I think of rainbows; it is a sign, a pact with creation.

Being human and easily titillated by gossip there were dozens of stories circulating on the *Willem Ruys* about shipboard romance. Our journey from Southampton to Singapore was scheduled to take six weeks. It is not possible to encapsulate men and women in such delightful surroundings without some sort of shipboard romance blossoming. All it takes is a glance across the dining table; a stroll to pause at the ship's rail and gaze up at the tropical starlit night, with offshore breezes bringing the tantalising trace of the perfume of cloves, cardamoms and vanilla. Shipboard romance is like a summer love affair; knowing that it has to end lends a sweet ecstasy, exquisite urgency and the smarting sting of knowing one has to leave the ship. Women separated from their husbands, men separated from their wives. Inevitably, the unattached men, the men without wives or fiancées were the more predatory. An elegant liner, on a magical tropical evening, gently ploughing the waters and disturbing the glittering ocean-path to an enormously bright moon is enough to make men forget their attachments and move in for the kill, some of them cruising like Zambesi crocodiles along the bank, ready to snap at any pretty little fawn that gently ventures into the water to drink.

One of the favourite stories that circulated in the second-class lounge when we left Medan was about a young Dutch wife who had sailed from Amsterdam to join her husband in Singapore. Apparently, she was involved in a most torrid love affair with one of the crocodiles—the ship's second officer. It was said, by the two elderly sisters who had saved all their lives for the trip, that the lovers were inseparable. They had been seen kissing, and much more, on the promenade deck, under the lifeboats and even in the bar at the after end of the ship. Recently, it was reported that the second officer only ever emerged from the lady's cabin to take his turn of duty on the bridge. It had been noticed that he was even absent from his duties in the dining room.

This young lady's husband must have been a romantic young man who loved his wife dearly. He arranged with the shipping company in Singapore to join the ship in Medan and sail the last part of the voyage from Medan to Singapore together with his wife. This information he kept to himself. He wanted to surprise his wife in the hope that she would think of him as a romantic and impetuous young man willing to find innovative ways of showing his love for her. When he joined the ship in Medan, no one knew of his coming. He registered as a passenger and picked up a key to his wife's cabin from the purser. When he located the cabin he gently inserted the key and let himself quietly in. He wanted nothing to spoil the surprise. This version of the subsequent events, I heard at the lunch table. Apparently, shortly after the husband let himself into his wife's cabin the Second Officer emerged, fairly quickly, with a bleeding nose and in a dishevelled state, hastily pulling on his tropical uniform shirt.

When this piece of news flew round the ship we all wanted a glance of them, a chance to send her, at least, a stern judgemental look. Hoping to catch sight of them in the bar or at lunch we waited with considerable excitement to see how she would cope with this situation. Husband and wife left the ship in Singapore, hand in hand, heads held high. However, it was reported that she had very red eyes.

Someone once said to me, "Remember young Thorp, never send your wife on an ocean liner by herself." The source of this wisdom, an elderly Planter took a sip from his whisky, he looked at me across the top of his glass. "Must be something to do with the movement of the ship, they all go off the handle."

"Really," I replied, "What about us? What about us men? Can we go on an ocean trip without our wives."

"Ah, young Thorp," he replied. "Now that's an entirely different thing."

The python on the train

One story I was told, was when a group of bachelors from the tin mine at Sungai Lembing had been down to visit Maurice Cotterill on the rubber estate at Panching. They had arrived in the afternoon and been out on the estate and along the jungle edge hunting wild boar without success. However, they had come across a sizeable python, which was still sleepy and inactive after its last meal. They found a box and somehow managed to lift the snake inside. Once they had it in the box not one of them really knew what they would do with it. So they carried it back to Cotterill's bungalow where they left it outside with a weight on the lid. That evening they all had a wonderful chicken curry prepared by Cotterill's cook and consumed enormous quantities of Anchor beer, purchased duty-free from the tin mine concession godown.

They woke up late the following morning. They showered with cold water from the Shanghai jars placed on the cement floor bathrooms. For breakfast they had leftover curry and bread, drank some more beer and decided it was time to make their way back to Sungai Lembing. They needed time for the journey. The four of them had commandeered a railway trolley, a simple wooden platform with four heavy iron wheels. The trolley was foot-propelled or pushed along the narrow-gauge railway used for transporting the tin to the river barges at Pasir Kemudi.

On the way back to Sungai Lembing, they decided to select a particularly dense section of jungle and release the snake to new surroundings. Carefully, they loaded the box with the snake and enough bottles of beer to see them back home. Each of them sat at one corner of the trolley, they waved Cotterill farewell, and started the laborious business of pushing the vehicle along the track with their outside leg.

After passing Kolek, the railway line dipped down to the river and followed the bank for several miles through some dense primary forest. Most of the climb was completed so they decided it was time to stop for a beer and let the snake go. Derek Nattrass, a Jordie, decided that the event should be recorded and he reached into his bag for his camera. Alec Cowie, who was a tough New Zealander, said that he felt up to the business of coaxing the snake out of its box. Cautiously he released the catch and lifted the lid, peered in, gently grasped the snake behind its head and pulled it up out of the box to be photographed. With a surprisingly rapid and powerful twist of its head, the snake pushed the box off the trolley and sank its fangs into Cowie's forearm.

"Come on you bastards," he screamed. "Help me get the bloody thing off."

"Just hold on, Alec," Nattrass shouted, desperately cranking the film advance lever. "Just one more shot, just one more. I'll never get another chance like this."

CHAPTER 3

Arrival On Kuala Reman Estate

I stayed at the Adelphi Hotel in Singapore. In1956, it was years before the building was torn down for development. When I stayed there it was a beautiful, old-fashioned hotel situated immediately opposite St. Andrew's Cathedral. There was a message waiting for me with instructions to visit the Borneo Company offices, where I picked up an advance on my salary and air tickets to Kuantan via Kuala Lumpur. The following morning on 14th February 1957, I caught the early morning flight from Singapore to Kuala Lumpur. There was a short stopover at the old Kuala Lumpur airport before continuing on my journey to the east coast of Malaya.

During the stop over my brother, Jim, and his wife, Shirley came to meet me. He was serving in the British Royal Air Force and had managed to take time off from his duties in order for he and his wife to come and see me when the plane landed. They stayed and chatted during the time it took the aircraft to re-fuel and take on freight for the east coast. We talked, but my ears were so blocked from the flight on the old DC3 aircraft that my brother must have thought I was even more dim-witted than he remembered. Eventually, he gave me the advice of holding my nose and blowing. I blew down my nose until I was red in the face. However, blowing and swallowing hard seemed to make little impression. It is ridiculous, but the sharpest memory of that meeting, nearly 50 years ago, is that I had blocked ears and could hardly hear a thing, and I so wanted to talk to my brother.

In those days Kuantan airport was, quite simply, just an airstrip with a couple of crude half-timber, half-concrete buildings and a small control tower. There was limited space for freight storage and a tiny waiting room and check-in counter with an Avery weighing machine graduated in kilograms and pounds. There was no air-conditioning but there was an electric fan suspended from the ceiling. Incoming aircraft taxied to a halt on a concrete apron immediately in front of the tower. When I arrived in Kuantan for the first time and clambered out of the DC3 I was met by Maurice and Sybil Cotterill. The concrete apron in front of the buildings was as hot as the bottom of an oven, and the glare from the midday sun instructed me harshly on the need for dark glasses. Cotterill, I knew, from the London office, was approaching fifty-five. He was a tall, almost gangling but good-looking man, with slightly protruding teeth and silver-white hair. He had a serious, but oddly in-attentive look and appeared to suck in his cheeks as if clamping his front teeth together. Sybil was small and slightly heavy for her height, with a tiny face and a slight cast in one of her eyes. She wore a loose-fitting, long cotton dress and an unexpectedly vivid application of lipstick to the lips of her small mouth.

The Cotterills took me to the Kuantan Club where I was introduced to Bill Dobbie, a huge man with the puffy face of a boxer. He was the Manager of Jabor Valley Estate. Sitting with Bill Dobbie in the club was P.N. Sansom, an elderly retired planter who was thin and frail-looking, a man with a cough and a tin of Senior Service cigarettes always in his hand. As I discovered later, PN always wore a fresh pair of beautifully ironed khaki-coloured shorts. Because of the thinness of his legs, the shorts ballooned out at his knees. If you sat opposite him in the Club, it soon became apparent that because of the heat he had dispensed with underwear. The phenomenon was what Bill Dobbie fondly referred to as an equipment review. All the men who frequented the club knew of this unintentional display and, out of respect and love for PN, they would always suggest that ladies did not occupy a chair opposite him.

The Kuantan Club was so much more open and cheerful than it is today. There was no air-conditioning, so all the windows and the main entrance doors were left wide open to the weather. It was usually always cool inside the club building. Around noon, the hottest part of the day, the surrounding trees offered some shade and helped to create a light breeze that would blow through the whole building ruffling tablecloths in the dining section. On particularly hot days the light breeze was a welcome supplement to the down draft of the ceiling fans that whirred incessantly. When it rained, the club staff, often assisted by members, would race from window to window slamming shutters and closing the main doors but usually too late to prevent rain from soaking the furniture and rivulets of water coursing out over the base line of the badminton court.

The Club itself deserves its own written history. In the 1950s and 1960s, it was the centre of expatriate activity in the Kuantan district. All British civil servants, most resident expatriate commercial men and almost all of the European Planters were members. Some Malaysians were also members, usually top civil servants or important junior members of the Pahang Royal family. The Sultan was, of course, the honorary President and a portrait of The Sultan and his consort was displayed over the entrance doors. They stared disconsolately at portraits of Queen Elizabeth and the Duke of Edinburgh.

At that time, there were not many ordinary Malayan citizens who were elected to join. This sounds tremendously

Planters in the Kuantan Club, 1957. Left to right: Van Hoeven, Head Assistant, Jabor Valley Estate; George Wood, Head Assistant, Kuala Reman Estates; Maurice Cotterill, M.B.E. Manager, Kuala Reman Estates; Peter Stone, Assistant Manager, Jabor Valley Estate.

discriminatory, which is exactly what it is intended to be. When I first arrived in Kuantan the Europeans in residence there, and indeed in other parts of Malaya were mostly British, and they still thought of the Malays, the Chinese and the Indian local population as natives, an unfortunate word with a strong flavour of discrimination. Many of the Europeans who lived in Malaya before independence, but not all, had discriminatory and condescending attitudes towards the local population. In Pahang, the Kuantan Club was referred to as the European club by the locals, *Kelab Orang Puteh*, and probably had some very rude Malay, Tamil and Chinese nicknames. The Chinese were staunch members of their *bangsa* or *kongsi* houses; separate associations with their own club-houses for the Cantonese, the Hokkien and the Hainanese. The Indians, mostly Tamils, were energetic members of the Kuantan Recreation Club and met for social and friendly contact at Indian temple events in Bukit Ubi Road. The Malays, of course, had the mosque and the *surais* or prayer houses where they met to gossip, meet their friends, discuss politics, as well as pray.

Happily, just as the plane landed in Kuantan, I managed to clear my pressure-blocked ears. This was fortunate because during the drive from the airport to Kuantan I was the subject of careful interrogation by my Manager's wife. Cotterill himself was taciturn and quiet, almost disinterested; but she was keen to know something of my background. I suppose, like most British people working in Malaya at that time, she wanted to weigh me up and know in which social box I would be placed.

We arrived at the Kuantan Club and stayed there for what seemed to me to be an interminably long time. We were settled in, a group of six people around a glass-topped table. And here we stayed until Maurice had had sufficient beer to reach the stage where he started pulling and toying with the grey chest hair that showed above the buttons of his shirt. I only ever knew Maurice to drink beer, never whisky or gin, but it did not take very many bottles of Anchor or Tiger before his speech was difficult to understand. It was usually at this point in time that Sybil prevailed and patiently shepherded him into their Rover car with the help of its even more patient Tamil driver, Ramasamy.

Those who know the road to Sungai Lembing today, in its present relatively wide and surfaced form, would find it difficult to imagine the state of the road in those days. It was more of a riverbed, full of potholes and gullies where the monsoon rains had scoured channels and destroyed culvert pipes. It was best to keep one's mouth shut tight in order to avoid biting the tongue as the car dropped into one of those sump-cracking holes. Heading for the estate for the very first time I was excited, of course, and full of questions; young and keen to show my awareness and curiosity. The Cotterills were both subdued and sleepy, he, tired and irritable with his beer, and Sybil just floating nicely with her gin. They were both reluctant to converse, and I felt somehow that I should not engage in conversation with the driver. We zig-zagged along the road being bumped and jolted for eighteen miles towards Sungai Lembing and my new home. Full of hope and expectation, I goggled at the enormous jungle trees, the wicked-looking swamps, intermittent fields and orderly rows of elephant-footed rubber trees.

When we arrived at the large but somewhat foreboding manager's bungalow at Panching an hour or so later, I was directed to a downstairs room. The bungalow was situated on a small hill; it was an unattractive two-storey wooden building painted weathered cream, equipped with Cuprinox-green shutters instead of windows. The downstairs shutters were slatted wooden doors, which opened up during the day to let in light and air.

The Chinese cook, who was tiny, with a parchment yellow skin tone and dressed in enormous white shorts, served me a lonely meal. Neither Maurice nor Sybil showed up for dinner. I suddenly felt very far from home, washed over in waves of homesickness and somehow confined to my room and the sparsely furnished downstairs lounge. I was also somewhat concerned because the wall planking of my room stopped about six inches from the floor, so that there was a considerable gap right around the room. I imagined, and feared, that all sorts of creatures would be sliding, slithering and running in and out of that gap during my sleep.

At about 9:00 pm, the cook knocked on the door with a bottle of water and a small kerosene lamp with a small glass funnel chimney and a round metal reflector with a picture of a beautiful Chinese girl looking over the top of a fan. I did not understand much of what he said to me, and I think he understood even less of what I said to him.

At exactly 10:00 pm, the diesel-driven generator coughed a couple of times, then cut out altogether. The single electric light in my room quickly dimmed into a red glow that faded entirely as the revs on the engine died away. The night suddenly became frighteningly silent, and at the same time, disconcertingly full of noise.

I lit the small kerosene lamp and wrote in my diary: "February 9th, 1957. Arrived at Panching to start my 4-year contract, 1,459 days to go!"

The explosions started just after I had carefully climbed onto a lumpy and damp-smelling single bed. Meticulously, I tucked the mosquito net under the mattress all round the bed and sat petrified staring out into the gloom of the poor light offered by the kerosene lamp. My God, I thought, it must be gunfire or mortars. It must be Communist terrorists (CT for short). Perhaps they were making an attack on the estate, or the explosions must be the Security Forces shooting off some warning shells. I decided that it would be best to extinguish the miserable little flame just in case a CT decided to walk around the bungalow later that evening. At least if there was no light in my room, then the CT would find it more difficult to catch sight of me through the enormous cracks in the wooden shutters.

Eventually, I dropped off into a fitful sleep. I was exhausted by an eventful day and burdened by an over-active imagination that was triggered off every time I heard an explosion. The trouble was that the explosions seemed to be all around the estate; some were very distant and some quite close to the bungalow. However, I took heart from the fact that the Cotterills were obviously not worried as I could not hear a single soul scrambling about in the caverns of the bungalow above my head, and the cook was not screaming in Chinese and running around pointing to where I was sleeping in order to save his own skin.

I met a morose and obviously slightly hungover Maurice Cotterill at 5:00 am the following morning. I knew that muster, or role call, was at 5:15 am and I was desperate not to be late on my first day at work. Maurice did not appear to want to speak to me, so I did my best to keep silent. However, I thought it was absolutely necessary to mention the gunfire of the night before. So, in my best conversational and man of the world manner I asked: "Was there much communist activity last night, or was it just a usual night?" He looked at me across the glass-topped rattan table. His lips pursed and his grey penetrating eyes regarded me with little affection.

"Communist activity?" he demanded.

"Yes," I replied. "I thought I heard mortars or light artillery firing. It was on almost all night. Quite kept me awake." I added.

"Mortar fire? Artillery? Those explosions are the Loosco bangers. They keep the elephants out of the re-plantings." I subsequently became very familiar with the Loosco banger; a calcium carbide-operated plunger arrangement with a fierce spring mechanism creating an enormously loud explosion. But I have always felt that, perhaps, the Cotterills could have warned me about them, before I went to bed.

Maurice downed his coffee and shot out of his chair without another word. I followed him and sat next to him in the Land Rover and we drove off into the chilly five-o-clock in the morning pre-dawn of a rubber estate in British Malaya. He stopped at the packing shed, where a dark figure of a man ran out of the building with a slip of paper called the muster chit. The Manager, the *tuan besar*, studied the piece of paper to see where and how many labourers were doing jobs in different parts of the estate. Then he called for Thomas, a young and lanky dark-skinned Malayali Indian. He turned to me in the Land Rover and said, "Go with Thomas. He'll show you round." I sat for a couple of seconds, not quite realising that I had been dismissed in a most callous and offhand manner. I climbed out of the vehicle, but before I could walk around the back of the Land Rover to meet Thomas, Cotterill drove off, crashing his gears as he picked up speed.

I shook hands with Thomas and said, "How do you do Mr Thomas. My name is Michael Thorp."

"Yes Sir," he responded. "We have all been told of your coming." As it happened, Cotterill's abrupt and almost hostile manner made me feel like an unwanted package that he wanted to pass on to Thomas as quickly as possible. However, it was the best thing he could have done. Thomas, over the next few months, helped me to start to learn my job. He was patient, respectful and knowledgeable. To this day I regret that he did not become my friend. But in those days, an expatriate Assistant Manager did not mix in a warm or social manner with the junior staff, who made up the team of local executives.

Melvin Gordon's elephant

I am reluctant to tell this story because there is an element of butchery of which I am not proud. About six months after I arrived in Malaya, a young Scot, Melvin Gordon also joined the expatriate staff of the estate. When I heard that he was coming I felt slightly put out, as true to the system, I had started to enjoy the fact that I was next in line after George Wood. Melvin was short and solid without being fat; he was a hard, jovial young man, perhaps a couple of years older than I. Where I was serious and cautious, Melvin was laughing and willing to give anything a try.

Melvin had been in the country about six months and had adapted to the business of being an Assistant Manager with alacrity and some style. His jovial nature made everyone smile and his open and easy-going manner induced the Panching labour force to become genuinely fond of him in a way I would never achieve.

Melvin threw himself with great energy into the task of chasing off elephants. One morning I met him when I was on my way to Sungai Lembing with a tractor power-drive, which was to be repaired.

"Last night the bastards wiped out about three acres of RP7 (Replant 7)." He thundered, "Beautiful four-year-old rubber trees. The elephants just uprooted them," he declared indignantly. "It looks as if they went along, row by row, and just pulled the bloody trees right out of the ground." I had called into Panching for a quick chat at the weekend. I was on my way to play cricket and spend a night in Sungai Lembing in John Burn's bungalow.

The next day, a Saturday, it was discovered that the elephants had again caused enormous damage in the same area of the replant, and despite dozens of people banging on metal latex collection buckets, the elephants refused to move out of the clearing and retreat into the jungle. One particular elephant started to behave very aggressively and made charges in the direction of a group of tappers who were vigorously banging their buckets. The animal clearly showed little fear of human beings.

Melvin decided it was expedient and necessary to shoot the elephant, a fairly large male. However, the only weapon he had to hand was a shotgun that belonged to the watchman. I do not know what sort of shot he used. I shudder to think that he may have used bird shot, or shot for small game. It took seventeen cartridges before the animal was finally dead. I have a photograph of Melvyn posing on one knee in front of the poor beast, one hand on the elephant, the other holding the shotgun.

Viapuri, an elderly Indian from south India, a Tamil or a Telegu, was Melvin's gardener. He gouged out the elephant's eyes the very same afternoon, shortly after the animal died. Viapuri was half blind. He cooked a soup made with the elephant's eyes in the belief that the power of sight, or improved sight, would flow into him with every spoonful he could eat.

The testicles, the scrotum and the penis disappeared sometime during the first night, and whoever performed that awful butchery had quite a task. When finally weakened, the elephant had collapsed and died on its knees. In order to cut out the genitals it had been necessary to push the animal onto its side, and then prop

Melvyn Gordon 1959, with the elephant he shot using a 12-bore shotgun and 17 cartridges. The elephant was threatening tappers and damaging replants.

up one of the hind legs with a trestle made of saplings cut from the surrounding secondary jungle.

I have no idea what happened to the tusks. People from Panching, and perhaps from the surrounding kampungs more or less helped themselves. The hair from the tip of the tail was taken, and various slices of fat and meat were removed from the back. Eventually the tappers working in the mature rubber along the edge of the replanting where the elephant was lying were allowed to tap other tasks. The stench of the rotting elephant could be picked up on the wind miles away. I suggested digging a pit and burying it. But George Wood was unwilling to pay for that work. The job would have had to be done by manual labour, as we had no bulldozers or tractors with diggers.

During my second visit to the corpse, driven by curiosity to again view the animal's body perhaps a fortnight after Melvin had shot it, I was revolted to see a monitor lizard, bloated and slimy with fat and fluids from the rotting carcass, emerge from a monstrous hole in what was left of the elephant's stomach.

Viapuri's sight did not improve.

Melvin had a bad time with the Game Department. The Game Rangers were not willing to accept that the elephant posed a danger. It was necessary for Melvin to document the damage done to the estate and set up costs to show that the investment in time, labour, clearing and replanting and lost income for the time the damaged area was out of production, together with the need to re-supply new trees was sufficient to warrant what he termed 'deterrent culling'. Somewhere in the Pahang Game Department records, if not already destroyed or eaten by white ants, there should be a report from Melvin attempting to justify the slaughter, but at the same time apologising for taking the law into his own hands. He was probably saved, that is, kept his job, because there was still a British Game Warden in charge of the Pahang Game Department at the head office in Temerloh.

CHAPTER 4

Life On A Rubber Estate

How was it to live life on a rubber estate in early 1957? Well, of course it was much easier in 1957 than it was in 1937, and in 1937 it was much, much easier than it was for those European pioneer Planters who started clearing land in the first part of the 20th century, 1900 and onwards. How was life on a rubber estate? It is a question I have been asked throughout my life when people hear that I was a planter. The quick answer is, that it was a desperately lonely life. Perhaps it is not possible to put into words the degree of loneliness I felt, at least during my first tour of duty.

The period of contract was four years without home leave. A four-year period of time during which it was assumed by my employers that I would remain in an innocent state of celibate learning, rather like a noviciate monk at the beginning of his call. However, being an assistant manager was not for me a call, although I wanted to be good at my job, but there was a clause in the contract specifically prohibiting marriage during the first tour. With hindsight, I understand the reasoning for such a tough clause, but in reality it was a misguided policy. During that first contract, a young planter either made it, or did not make it. It was a policy of make the grade, or get out. It is correct, at least in this day and age, to say such terms of service are totally unreasonable, almost inhuman. There were many casualties. Also many success stories, and perhaps many of the men who in the days before the Second World War went through even stricter regimes; for example, seven-year contracts, will, if they are still alive, expostulate that it never did them any harm. I am certain that young Malaysian planters today would never consider such terms.

The cost of sending young British expatriates out to a rubber estate in Malaya in the days when cheap air passages were not available was an economic item to be seriously considered. It usually took up to a month for the journey out to Singapore from Europe. Paying for the cost of the passage and paying a salary to a young man who knew nothing of the business of being a planter was an expensive investment. It was also a chancy investment. Not all of them were suited to the life of a planter and and therefore did not last the course. However, some young men felt that once they had started, they had to stay on, even though they hated the job. They were kept in harness from a sense of sticking things out, not wanting to disappoint parents and friends by returning to Britain after only a few months. In addition, they were kept in the job until their four years were up, because of the clause in their contract about passage money. If a young British planter felt that he had made a mistake, and resigned, he had to pay the full cost of his passage home to Britain together with the proportionate cost of his passage out to Malaya, in terms of the unserved months of contract remaining. For example, if you were employed, as I was, on a four-year contract and you resigned after two years, you would have to pay your own fare home plus half of the cost of getting you out to the estate in the first place.

A planter, or manager, in those days had almost the power of life and death with regard to the labourers on the estate. The same power was exercised over the executive staff, the conductors and the office clerks, the teachers in the estate schools and the dressers in the estate hospital. All were accountable to the manager—the *Tuan Besar*, or in Tamil, the *Peria Dorai*. I am not proud of this, nor am I ashamed. This is simply a statement of how things were set up at that time. This was the system that I was drawn into on my very first day at work on Kuala Reman Rubber Estate at Panching.

Everything and everyone depended on the manager. There was little chance of appeal against his decision, and, if a labourer was fired and termed a bad hat, then his chances of getting work on one of the other European controlled estates in the district were not particularly good.

For the labour force and the staff, the manager was the equivalent of Managing Director, Bank Manager, Agriculturist, Chemist, Mechanical Engineer, Medical Adviser, Family Counsellor, Father Figure, the Giver Away of Prizes, King Solomon in family disputes and the Source of all things: work, sick-pay, maternity leave, a house to live in, miserable as it most certainly was, a crèche where one could place one's child when working, and medicine when one was sick. For the average estate labourer one could say that it was a living, miles away from the nearest town, subject to the threat of snake-bite, attacks by wild pig, getting trampled on by elephants, and on some occasions, being attacked and eaten by a tiger.

I am horrified to say that on certain occasions Tamil labourers have thrown themselves down and grasped my feet saying, "*Tuan*, you are my father and my mother." A Malay or a Chinese would never do that. But the Tamil, at least in those days, knew that to throw oneself completely at the mercy of the Manager or the Assistant Manager in reality was only underlining the true situation. He or she saw the action as the ultimate bargaining position to avoid being sacked or fined or demoted.

In those days Malaya was more hostile to the Tamils. Somehow they were in the country on sufferance brought in from destitute families in villages in India by some contractor, who had long since disappeared. They knew nothing except estate life, or perhaps to work as labourers for the Public Works Department, breaking stone and carrying interminable loads of land fill in baskets on their heads. The Tamil estate labourer needed the security of the estate in an alien land. He needed the assurance and companionship of being with his own kind, other Tamils who could speak his own language. He needed the estate in order to have a place to perform *pujah* at the estate Hindu temple and he looked on the estate as his home, his village, his family—his everything. To be thrown off the estate was tantamount to disaster.

If things went badly for a Malay labourer he could always make tracks back to his kampong, his village. With the pride of a *bumiputra* ('son of the soil') and with a strong sense of belonging, he could always *pulang*, or return home. There in the *kampung*, without any difficulty, he could find a home. He could live with a friend, a cousin or his own immediate family. For sustenance he could fish in the river, snare birds, grow *keladi* and yam; he could work in the local paddy field, collect bund-side vegetables or undertake to watch over the headman's buffalo while they grazed, in return for an evening meal, a coffee and a *bidi* roll of tobacco. He could survive comfortably without the need to start a rigorous day's work at 5:00 am on a regimented estate run by the hateful *orang puteh*. If he lost his job... so what, he was a son of the soil; he belonged.

The labouring class Chinese were also imported into Malaya or made their own way into the country, but somehow they seemed to be much more resourceful, more withdrawn and self-reliant in their Chinese way of being.

Many of the older Chinese labourers, men and women alike, would only speak their own particular Chinese dialect, and gave the haughty impression of dismissing the Malay language as inferior; something they could not be bothered with. There would usually be some special reason for them to have taken a job as a tapper or a labourer on a rubber estate, a somewhat degrading occupation for someone with ambition and drive. It might have been because they could settle somewhere close to their family who could be engaged, perhaps, in shop-keeping activities, or driving a bus, or a timber lorry, or working for the tin mine at Sungai Lembing. The Chinese labourer looked on the estate as a source of income that would serve his interests until something better came along They had their networks, family, friends or someone who would fix them up with something. In addition to tapping rubber in the morning, they could grow vegetables in the afternoon until the opportunity came for them to go up to Sungai Lembing and get a job in the tin mine. They could travel across the state to a sawmill to work for a Chinese contractor, join in open-cast mining at Gambang or labour for better wages in the gold mines at Raub.

The Cantonese greeting of "*sik chaw meh*?" means, quite literally, have you eaten? Of course, it means more; it refers to general well-being and health—but, in their fundamental way, the Chinese know that all, health, happiness, a place to settle and eke out a living depends on food. In those early days, when Malaya was approaching independence from the British and also throwing off the iron grip of Chinese terrorists, it really meant something to ask, "*sik chaw meh*?" Even if a Chinese was starving, he would invariably reply, "*sik chaw*".

Because of the Emergency, there hung over each Chinese head the false spectre of 'collaborator', and this induced the Malayan Chinese to be even more careful with people they did not know. However, if a stranger did show up in a Chinese community he would usually bring greetings from a relative in another town or state, and in return he would receive a bowl of rice if food was available. A stranger, at that time was a useful bearer of news, of how things were in the village or town he had come from, and what conditions were like in the rest of the country. In this way, the Chinese built up an infallible intelligence service, an information chain that snapped up news of jobs, opportunities, projects, places to avoid and names that could be useful. These bonds were even stronger within the confines of the *kongsi*, the sleeping dormitories and labour lines or in the Chinese associations.

The British Planter in Malaya was the embodiment of Empire, power, money, privilege, and, hopefully, at least for the people on his estate, also a good-natured man. I was plunged into the supervision of all plantation activities: agricultural, manufacturing, water-supply, roads and bridges, transportation, education, training, welfare, infrastructure, policing, maintaining law and order, labour relations (now referred to as human resources) accounting, and an advisory role in everything from how to deal with marital problems to malaria control. At times it was a quite an impossible role to perform.

Primed by high commodity prices during the Korean War, rubber was in great demand. It was needed for tires, for industrial and military purposes, for medical appliances and as a waterproofing additive to garments. The industry was booming and the forecast for continued high market prices was buoyant. Many countries in South East Asia as well as India and Sri Lanka rushed to replant areas of old, uneconomic rubber as well as develop plantations from primary jungle.

The agricultural act of planting rubber trees, which involves the clearing of new land, usually secondary jungle, or replanting old stands of rubber trees in tropical countries such as Vietnam, Thailand, Burma, Sri Lanka, South India, Indonesia and Malaysia is seasonal. The different estate agronomical activities depend, to a large extent, on the weather. Although Malaysia has a tropical climate where temperature varies little throughout the year, the East Coast of peninsular Malaysia is subject to a marked rainy season referred to as the northeast monsoon. There is a dry season on the East Coast. The months from March to August can be quite arid. Rubber trees lose their leaves during February and March and this loss is referred to as 'wintering', although it has nothing to do with a drop in temperature. Wintering is followed by a period when the trees put on a new flush of leaves, and all this growth activity within the tree leads to a decline in latex yields.

It is during the rainy season, the monsoon, that one plants the rubber trees from the nurseries into the field, or, as was done in the 1950s, three germinated seeds were planted at each point throughout a field replant. This work was done in the rainy season to take full advantage of the moisture in the soil and obtain better growth results, or 'strike' in the field.

The dry season is the best time for preparation of land for planting, and is also the best time to clear drains, drain swamps or build roads. A young European, fresh out from Surrey, or even Fife for that matter, had to learn the cycle of clearing and weeding. Learn how to eradicate competitive weeds; understand the necessity for the sowing of interrow cover crops, and, just as the annual monsoon rains start or are expected to start, help supervise the taxing task of transporting the new young rubber plants out to the field. Endless rows of holes, the topsoil remixed with organic fertiliser, or rock phosphate. The rows, 30 feet apart and the planting holes, at eight or ten feet apart in each row. Planting distance, depended on dozens of factors: the bark renewal after tapping of the clone selected, whether one was using budded plants or selected seedlings, the tendency to snap in heavy winds, resistance to disease and other influences usually advised to the Planter by bulletins issued by the Rubber Research Institute of Malaya. It was recommended to plant up initially at 240 trees to the acre which would be thinned down to about 120 trees, when the trees are first opened up for tapping eventually arriving at an optimal final tapping stand of about 100 trees to the acre. Today, everything is measured and calculated on the metric system and rubber has given way to oil palm.

The rubber estate planting cycle takes a year, and it has to be experienced to understand how all the individual tasks fit into the major job of actually getting a cleared field planted up with selected new rubber trees. A young planter must learn exactly how the work is planned. Going through all the procedures just once is not enough, to learn. The jobs must be repeated, and that means going through the procedures year after year exactly as in any agricultural undertaking. It is a complicated pattern involving the need to coordinate labour requirements for surveying, lining, terracing, holing, fertilizer application and a hundred other jobs that need people who know what they are doing and have, over the years, achieved considerable expertise. In addition to new planting, or replanting, there is the main activity; the real business of producing rubber from the mature areas of the estate in order to generate the revenue to sustain the replanting cycle and make a profit in order to satisfy the shareholders.

In the tropics, with unbelievably heavy downpours of eroding rain, there are special dangers that are much more severe and require more special precautions than in a temperate climate. There is the problem of soil erosion, drainage and terracing, and the important requirement for cover crops to protect the soil, retain moisture and supply nitrogenous fertilizer. All these procedures, steps in successful estate husbandry, have to be understood and learnt. In those days, dealing with the Labour force was perhaps the most essential and difficult part of the job of being a planter. I am sure it is no different today in modern Malaysia where, to a large extent labour forces are recruited from Indonesia and Bangladesh, and the major crop planted in most estates or plantations is oil palms.

When I arrived, and indeed, during the first few weeks and months on the estate as a young British planter, the whole world of Malaya was vastly different to what I was used to from the deck of a ship or the comfort of Surrey. I certainly needed a lot of time to adjust. Firstly, I had to adjust to the climate. I also had to find my place within the expatriate community where I was very junior. I felt it was important to find my own style, my own way of being in a new world. I had to learn to fight my fears, which could involve everything from snakes, to being murdered in my bed by Communist Terrorists. I had to get over being homesick and missing friends and family. I needed time to find myself, to learn how to cope creatively with the loneliness. There was no television, no continuous electricity supply and, as a young, man there was a limit to the amount of radio interference I could tolerate. It was not easy to sit and read books about the English home counties or wild stretches of Yorkshire while sitting in sultry heat and slapping at mosquitoes. What should I do? Should I go hunting? The jingle surrounding the estate had a plentiful supply of wild boar, *kijang* and *pelandok*. Should I collect butterflies? Should I build a boat in my spare time, read all the books I could lay my hands on, listen to music? The nearest cinema was an hour's drive away in Kuantan, and it was equally far to the European Club in Sungai Lembing where, occasionally, there was a film. I had no transport of my own, no Land Rover or car, no motorcycle, not even a bicycle. If I needed to leave the estate I had to ask for transport. And my excursion would be combined with some other essential transport operation. Cotterill made it painfully clear that the estate vehicles were not to be considered as part of my convenience.

Although I have criticised the four-year contract, I needed much of that first four years to find out if being a rubber planter was the life I really wanted. Was being a planter what I really wanted to do for the next thirty-five years of my working life? In view of all the uncertainties and all the questions that I would inevitably ask myself time and time again; then, perhaps, four years was an appropriate term for a young man, straight off the ship from Britain, to learn his job.

In addition to learning the job, a young British planter was required to learn the language of the country, Malay, as well as the language of his own particular labour force. Most of the larger Agency houses who were in control of recruitment and the careers of planters made it a condition that the Incorporated Society of Planters examination in basic Malay should be passed during the first tour of duty. No pass, and the planter would not be invited back for a second tour of duty.

From about 1890–1930 , Britain desperately needed labourers in Malaya, Sri Lanka, East Africa and other colonies. In Malaya it was found that the Malays were too independent to want to buckle down to regular, tedious and indeed, poorly paid work as an estate labourer. There were similar reasons in Sri Lanka, where the Sinhalese considered themselves far above menial labouring tasks; and in Africa, where strong tribal influences precluded the African from buckling down to the tough discipline of plantation life. In India, particularly south India, the British were facing insurmountable problems of poverty and a destitute population. Recruitment for jobs overseas was considered an ideal solution. Accordingly, able-bodied South Indians were recruited on contract. Outlets in India collected together whole gangs of twenty, thirty or a hundred men and women at a time, and they were shipped out of places like Mandappam Camp as deck cargo on the way to British colonial destinations.

Arriving in Malaya for the first time, they saw little or nothing of the country or the cities. They were given no choice and were herded together in their contracted group and transported by buffalo cart, or by train and on the back of lorries to godforsaken destinations. They ended up on isolated estates to live in labour lines not much better than lean-to shelters. Not all labour forces were Indian Tamils. Some were recruited from the hill areas around Hassan and Chikmaglur and other places where they spoke Telegu. In the case of Nada Estate, Kolek, which was at that time one of the separate divisions of Kuala Reman Rubber Estates, quite a large proportion of the labourers were Chinese. They were surplus to the requirements of the tin mine at Sungai Lembing, overspill, people waiting for a better job, a better chance. When I was transferred to Nada, I started to learn Cantonese.

All those years ago, when the south Indians were shipped out from Tamil Nadu like cattle, the Tamils and Telegus were usually employed on a 10-year contract or, in some cases for even longer periods. The terms of South Indian labour contracts, if indeed they actually existed on paper, made the terms of my own contract look positively golden. However, as often as not, at the expiration of ten years the contractor who had employed the labourers was not to be found. Under the terms of the contract, the contractor was obliged to pay for steamer passage back to India. The contractor, having disappeared, left the labourers stranded with no savings, no job security and to a large extent entirely dependent upon the largess of the estate manager where they worked. And he, the English manager, hid comfortably behind the fact that the estate had at no time entered into a contract with the labourer—the labourer, poor fellow, actually had a contract with Mr Samiveloo or Mr Ramakrishnan, and unfortunately they had long since disappeared into comfortable shophouses up in the hills of Ootacamund.

When the manager asked his labourers where the contractor was at the end of their agreed period, he would get the reply from a *mandor*: "The blackguard bolted, Sir." So poor Ramasamy, Krishnan, Muthu or Vadiveloo having had, of course, absolutely no chance of saving any money during the ten years of labour was left high and dry. The cost of purchasing a deck passage on a steamer from Singapore or Penang bound for Madras was completely out of the question.

The vast majority of contract imported Tamils just continued to work on in Malaya, more or less trapped in a cycle of exploitation and poverty. In any event, what would they have gone back to in India? Who would want them? Who would employ them? India had more than enough of its own problems, its own over-abundance of destitute people trying to become a part of the Indian labour force looking for jobs. If labourers from Malaya did make the trip back to India, they ran the risk of ending up having to rely for food and shelter on their own already destitute relatives.

Eventually, the Tamil labourers who had been shipped to Malaya married, had children on the estate, ready to supply the next generation of labourers. The labour force and I had something in common. We were imported workers. The difference was that I lived in an enormous bungalow, had a servant, and a salary that was at least ten times more than they could earn. They were exploited, and I—as part of the management team was employed.

Today, I am delighted to witness how the vast majority of the descendants of Tamil contracted labourers have cast off the yoke of estate life. They have escaped from ignorance and menial labour by hard work and aptitude. Today's generations of Malaysian Tamils hardly ever look back to those unfortunates who passed through Mandappam Camp; who were shipped out on the decks of Straits steamship vessels; not by name but by tally, supplied with rice cooked in enormous black pots, bedded down under canvas tarpaulins and then herded like pliant, uncomplaining cattle to jungle destinations. We British have much to answer for.

Baby elephant

I know this story is true. I have lived in the bungalow where it happened and I have worked with George Wood.

In 1956, George was living his bachelor existence on Nada Estate, some 2,400 acres of land surrounded by almost primary jungle on the hilly approach to Sungai Lembing. The Nada bungalow was a huge, sad-looking two-storey building. Even though the majority of Planters' houses were often two-storey buildings, they were usually referred to as bungalows, a leftover colonial habit from an acquired Bengali word.

Nada Estate was very unkempt, overgrown and difficult. It was all old rubber planted from 1918–1924 at a time when the prospects for natural rubber were considered to be promising after the end of the First World War. During the worst part of the Communist Emergency in Pahang in 1948, the estate had been abandoned for more than a year. As a result, some parts of the estate, particularly the Ampang flats, were very badly upkept. The interrow areas were overrun with belukar, wild coffee and Siam weed. The undergrowth was so dense that the only way one could

Nada Estate, assistant manager's bungalow, 1960. The bungalow has been demolished and replaced by two staff buildings on what is now Kolek Estate, near Sungai Lembing.

get into the field was to follow the tappers' paths alongside the massive old rubber trees.

When the budget permitted, a brush cutter, towed behind an old Massey Ferguson tractor, would be sent in to clear the area in order to allow more sunlight and air to penetrate the dismal shade of rows of secondary jungle. Air and light also helped to prevent the development and spread of mouldy rot on the tapping panels. However, there were so many drains and areas of swamp that large parts of Ampang were virtually pockets of impenetrable secondary jungle. This was ideal country for wild pigs and the area was criss-crossed with many tracks made by wild elephants in their ceaseless searching for food. When I worked on Nada Estate there were many elephants, at that time they were almost abundant in that part of Pahang.

The elephants followed a track out of the Ampang flats and around Charu Field 7 hill where the Manager's bungalow was *situated. One evening in December 1956, the monsoon rain, which had been pouring down for the best part of the day eased off, and George Wood was pleased to get some relief from the constant noise of rain falling on the corrugated iron roof of the bungalow. In the relative quietness, he heard what sounded like an animal bellowing and the voice of a very excited cook calling him from the top of the stairs.*

"Tuan, Tuan," *called the agitated Chinese cook,* "Satu anak gajah adah-la masok di-dalam kebun Tuan. Belakan pagar." *A baby elephant had wandered away from the heard and got itself caught up inside the high barbed wire security fence surrounding the bungalow. George could hear mature elephants trumpeting for the baby to catch up. They seemed to be moving down the hill towards the Charu River. George grabbed a flashlight and went out into the garden to explore. Pushing against the fence, desperately trying to move off in the direction of its mother, the baby was injuring itself against the spikes of wire that were supposed to keep Communist terrorists out of the compound.*

The tiny elephant had wandered through the always-open main gate and followed the fence to the rear of the bungalow. When George flashed his light onto the small creature, it was obviously desperately trying to follow its mother but was prevented by the fence between them. George thought it looked rather like a puppy on a leash getting caught up on the wrong side of a lamp post. Neither the mother nor the baby understood the predicament, and the mother continued moving away down the hill with the rest of the herd.

The beam of George's torch temporarily arrested the baby's desperate efforts at pushing through the fence. When it gazed in a bemused way into the beam of the torch, George noted where the baby elephant had caused the fence to bulge outwards, and he could clearly see blood trickling down from its head into the baby elephant's eyes. Caught in the fence and staring up at George along the beam of light, it bleated and bellowed as it heard its mother's cries getting further and further away.

George said that for a few moments he had no idea what to do. But he did not want the baby to continue hurting itself by pushing into the barbed wire. He decided to put it in the garage. Gingerly placing his arms around the tiny animal's neck and shoulders, George leaned into the animal and half-pulled and half-pushed it into the garage. "I made encouraging motherly sounds," George used to say, when telling the story in his strong Fifer accent. George said it was an amazing experience. The tiny animal, which only came up to George's waist in height, apparently registered no fear of George or of the cook, who kept making rapid fluttery movements with a tea towel. Having got the animal into the garage, George grabbed the tea towel and wiped away the blood. He was pleased to see that the wounds did not appear to be serious; mostly small puncture marks and very little tearing. George said he was amazed at just how hairy the baby elephant was, with coarse rough black hair, almost like bristles.

George told the cook to quickly make some warm powdered milk and put it into a beer bottle. "Dengan banyak gula jugaat." Add plenty of sugar, he instructed the cook. Waiting for the milk, George discovered that the baby was a male when it wet his feet with a surprisingly warm stream of urine.

The baby elephant just loved the milk and George sent the cook back for more. By the end of the second bottle the baby decided that George was quite the best thing in the whole of the jungle. He nuzzled up to George and leaned into him in a most affectionate manner. "Ah, he smelled so good," George would say, "like a very young calf. You know, sort of milky and warm and clean." For those

of us who knew George, this was an unusual side to his normally
bluff bachelor character.

Eventually, of course, the elephant mother returned. When
she did, she was most perturbed. She followed her own footsteps
but crashed into the garden by simply putting her weight on the
wooden uprights supporting the fence. Fortunately, George and the
cook had heard her coming, so they left the garage door wide open
and the cook hastily retreated up the concrete steps to the bungalow.
Before following him, George tried pushing the baby in the direction
of its mother. But this caused the mother to rush up the garden
towards George and bang her trunk on the roof of the garage. George
immediately abandoned his baby and ran up the steps, three at a
time, to what he fervently hoped would be the safety of the bungalow.
The mother trumpeted at the baby to come away from the garage.
George said the baby was so full of milk that all it probably wanted to
do was to sleep for a few hours. The mother half-pulled her offspring
and, according to George, smacked him a few times with her trunk
at the same time, pushing him ahead of her down the drive, past
the bungalow and out of the gate.

For many years after, whenever the incident was talked about
in the Club, it was referred to as 'George's Baby'. It was a favourite
topic, sometimes trotted out to spellbind newcomers to the Kuantan
Club and the European Club in Sungai Lembing. And George would
be pointed out to spellbound listeners. When they asked him if he
was the man who had a baby elephant in his garage, George, who
eventually wearied off the story, would say laconically, "Aw, that was
a long time ago". As if many other interesting events had happened
to him since then.

CHAPTER 5

Working With Robbie And The Elephant fence

One beautiful morning, I had been out on an inspection round with Mr Thomas. He had taken me in the small punt-like boat over to the North Division. It was a wild area of land to the north of the Kuantan River, and comprised of some 400 acres of almost abandoned old rubber trees. The trees were being tapped, but on payment of very high rates per pound of latex, this was to encourage the tappers to work and move around in such a wild place.

Thomas and I were walking along the northern boundary following a slashed path that afforded us a view of the dense growth along the edge of the jungle. The air was scintillating with droplets of moisture reflecting the sun, and heady with the delicate scent of pigeon orchids. They were festooned in epiphytic clusters on the old trees, the flowers hanging down in white cascades. Immediately before the flowers open, they look like hundreds of miniature white pigeons perching on the clusters of the hanging orchid stems. Pigeon orchids have a short life span; they last for just one day. When their flowers open up to the sun, the areas of the estate where they bloom are suddenly transformed into perfumed gardens, and the exquisite scent of forever imprints on the senses a forlorn and deep desire to experience that smell once again.

Suddenly, Thomas grabbed my arm and cautioned me to be still. I was expecting a snake or a scorpion or even one of the monstrous spiders I had observed. I looked in the direction he was pointing to, with his outstretched hand, to see a herd of elephants. We were very close to them. I guessed that they were some fifty or seventy yards away from us, standing just outside the jungle edge. There was one enormous tusked animal and four large elephants together with a youngster and a tiny baby.

"Must be careful, Sir," Thomas hissed. "With babies they are very dangerous." Thomas refused to allow me to shift to a closer position to get a better view. It was not until the elephants started moving away from us that he decided we should turn back and retrace our footsteps rather than continue our inspection along the same path ahead of us into some heavy *belukar*.

I was delighted to have seen them, and naturally, at breakfast with Sybil Cotterill later that morning I told her of our close meeting with the elephants. "You are a very lucky young man," she said, fluttering her eyelids in her own very particular way. "You know, some people have been living in Malaya for years and have never seen an elephant." She looked at me, and remained silent as if considering the wisdom of her next statement. "I have never seen a wild elephant, and I have lived on a rubber estate for many years."

Later that afternoon, I was in the office struggling with the complexities and terrors of the check roll, and wilting under the heat. Quite suddenly, a green Land Rover with the Pahang Coat of Arms emblazoned on the door panels came to a dusty halt right in front of my office door, which was fully open to catch any cooling breezes. The vehicle brought with it a cloud of red, laterite dust, which was one of the reasons Cotterill did not allow vehicles to drive right up to the office. A well-built European with broad shoulders and a striking, ginger-streaked moustache, jumped out of the driver's seat. At the same time, three uniformed Malay men climbed out of the back, carrying rifles and shotguns.

The European strode into my office. "Hallo," he boomed and stuck out his hand. "I'm Robbie. Is Maurice here?" I stuttered my own name and showed him into Maurice's office. Robbie strode past me and shook Cotterill's hand. "Maurice! You old bastard! Have you got a beer? My throat's as dry as a camel's arse." This was my first meeting with Mr A.K. Robinson, Game Warden, Pahang.

At breakfast the following morning I was instructed by Maurice to follow Mr Robinson into Replant 4 (RP4) and assist him in every possible way. Maurice went on to explain that Robbie was going to introduce us on the estate to a new type of electric fence. He was going to show us how erect an elephant fence, a type of fence used in Africa, to good effect. "He's a bit of a colourful chap," said Maurice. "But you can learn a great deal from him."

I walked the two miles out to RP4 in what was now yet another sappingly hot day, with a blazing sun high in the sky. I was dressed in Maurice's dress code, which was shorts, a short-sleeved cotton shirt, and brownish-coloured field boots or basketball boots manufactured by Bata. In addition, I had a walking stick. This was also a copied trait from Maurice; it was seldom used as a support, but it gave a comforting feeling of having some protection, should an angry cobra suddenly decide to strike. In all my years in Malaya, it never occurred to me to seek shade from the sun, or wear a hat, or, stupidly, take a bottle of water with me into the field.

Waiting in the burning hot sun for Robbie to turn up at the appointed hour, I eventually had to seek some relief from the heat. As 12:00 pm came and dragged past in the staccato whine of grasshoppers, I looked for cover in the shade of the old stand of rubber running down the side of RP4. The delayed appointment with Robbie taught me that this man was far too colourful and important to be locked into punctuality when dealing with one of Maurice Cotterill's creepers, or junior assistants. I also assumed correctly, as it turned out, that I would certainly hear about it if I should ever be late for an appointment with him. This flamboyant Game Warden, with his gingery boyish hair and bushy moustache turned up at a quarter to two. He jumped out of the Land Rover and immediately commenced barking out orders in the Malay language. I could tell that he spoke a beautiful Malay. Even at that early stage of my career, I could hear that his intonation and fluency far-surpassed that of my own manager. I sulked. I thought the least he could do was apologise for his lateness, and for keeping me from lunch. Sulking was a waste of time. He barked a few more instructions, heartily clapped the Tamil *mandor* in charge of the labourers on the back, ignored me completely and drove off in his usual cloud of insensitive dust.

I worked for a week on the elephant fence. In principle, it was an electric fence, but with insulators affixed to the inside of the fence posts. The thick electric wire was threaded through the insulators in one continuous line, the theory being that if an elephant came up against the wire and moved forward, then it would continue to experience a rapid series of electric shocks. The wire would move forward with the elephant, and, in theory, would not break because of the small amount of slack between all the posts. The wire, rather than snapping, was supposed to 'give' as the beast moved forward into the replant. At 24 volts a shock, it was hoped that the animal would decide it prudent to retreat. Eventually, we had the whole clearing of 212 acres surrounded by fence posts, with all the insulators in place, and the heavy-gauge wire threaded through and joins in the wire were hammered flat and filed smooth so could they would not jam or be halted in the insulator holes.

The fence never really worked. Not efficiently, and certainly it was not cost-effective. There were too many factors against it, and elephants are not like domesticated horses, cattle or sheep.

In the early stages, when we were all supervising the new fence, 'Robbie's fence' as it was known, worked. Ismail, the watchman, explained that the elephants were nowhere near RP4 during the first couple of weeks, so the fence was never put to any real kind of test. I knew that at least one small herd of the local elephant population was busy on the North Division, where Thomas and I had seen them. Some three weeks, after the fence was completed, the elephants moved south across the river in the direction of RP4. Ismail knew of this and was carefully following them. He told me, through an interpreter, that one evening a baby elephant had walked calmly, and without experiencing a shock, under the fence. Its mother followed the calf and obviously received a shock which, Ismail reported, made her shake her head from side to side, and pick up a at crashing speed to join her calf. The wire snapped and the circuit was broken. This was explained to Maurice, who disliked bad news and became unfairly furious with Ismail. Maurice ordered the wire to be repaired, which I supervised. But it snapped again the next morning. We gave up the idea of electrical fencing when the elephants started pulling up the fence posts along with the three-year-old rubber trees of RP4. "Robinson can bloody well come up and shoot one of them," Maurice barked at me. "Don't spend any more money on that damned fence."

During the whole eight months that I worked for him, Maurice never chose to actually talk to me, or listen to anything I had to say, or give me words of friendly or even fatherly advice. He was fifty-four when I arrived on the estate. He retired shortly after his fifty-fifth birthday and moved to Cheshire to breed

Cinchilla rabbits. Maurice simply did not want to have to deal with me or have the responsibility of employing me, or the other British Assistants who joined Kuala Reman shortly after my arrival.

Maurice more or less told me, in very plain language, that Mr Lawrence, a Malayali Indian and a senior conductor, was worth five of me. Mr Lawrence was on leave in India when I arrived. Maurice kept referring to Lawrence as his right-hand man. With hindsight, I think Maurice had probably recommended that Lawrence be promoted up to Assistant Manager's level. But, instead of listening to Cotterill's views, the Board in London had incorrectly, in Maurice's view, chosen to employ a twenty-year-old English ignoramus who needed total instruction in everything. Maurice certainly did not want the responsibility of having a young, untrained Englishman on his estate. An Englishman who could not speak Malay, who knew nothing of tapping panels and preventing wounds, who could not tell pink disease in young rubber from athletes foot. In short, my Manager did not want me on the estate. It was reported to me that he said in the Club one day, "I don't have the time and patience to train up young creepers, hardly out of nappies. I'm leaving the country. I'm retiring after thirty-five years of planting. I am not the man to train these snotty young men, and it is unreasonable of The Board to send them out to me."

Of course, I wanted to challenge his attitude. Ask him exactly how he came to learn his job when he arrived on his first estate. But I never did. I knew that his generation had experienced much tougher conditions, with even longer contract periods, in some cases seven years. I assumed therefore, that Maurice had learned the job of 'planting' the hard way, and if I challenged him, I would be back on an aircraft in the direction of Singapore, with no written testimonial in my pocket and the ignominy of having been sacked.

I met Robbie a few weeks after his fence was abandoned. We were in the Kuantan Club. I had just been accepted as a member and had my own book that I could sign for drinks and food. It was one of my very first excursions away from the estate and down to Kuantan on my own. I had escaped from the protective skirts of Sybil and the disdainful eye of my constantly unfriendly boss. When we discussed 'Robbie's fence', Robbie blamed the watchman. "Of course it was the bloody watchman. Wasn't doing his job," Robbie said. He sat slumped in a chair, with the ever-present Chinese hand towel, embroidered with the words "Good Morning" at both ends, thrown over his shoulder. "That bugger of a watchman thinks that if my fence works, as it bloody well should have done, he'll be out of a job." He leaned forward in his chair and said, in a darkly conspiratorial manner, "And if Auntie Maurice thinks I'm going up to Panching to shoot one of those elephants, he's got another think coming." I subsequently came to learn that Robbie was passionately fond of wild elephants, and he was a great conserver of all Malaya's wild life a well as an excellent game warden. He had, over the years, been forced to shoot elephants and tigers and other animals that were making life for *ulu* dwellers and villagers impossible. But he hated it when he pulled the trigger and his staff said he wept when he went up to touch the animals immediately after the kill.

It was in connection with Robbie that I had one of my first meetings with Peter Stone. Peter was also a planter; he was working on Jabor Valley Estate, the most southerly section of Terrenganu that sticks down into Pahang, which on the map looks like a dog's cock. A few years older than I was, Peter was very senior in terms of the number of years he had been in Malaya, as he had taken part in the war against communist terrorists as an officer in the British Army before starting out as a planter. Peter often took the trouble to explain to me many of the facts of Malayan life. In the Club one late afternoon, Robbie had been talking about his air-hostess, and how he would have to get a move on, leave the Club and pick her up before flying his aircraft back to Kuala Lumpur. I sat listening to this wildly romantic figure of a man relating stories of air-hostesses, and flying light aircraft in difficult conditions. At each exploit, my jaw dropped and my eyes were as wide-open as only fresh-in-Malaya-twenty-year-old eyes can get. When Robbie left us, I turned to Peter and said, "My God, has he got his own air-hostess?"

"Don't be a silly sod," Peter replied. "It's only Ramlah, and she's a taxi-dancer from the Bukit Bintang dance hall in KL. She comes from Ayer Puteh, just up the road here, so he gives her a lift back to Kuantan in a plane he hires from the KL Flying Club. She goes to see her mother, and he, crafty old goat, gets an accompanied passage."

Wilf Johns and the tiger

I heard this story from Wilf Johns himself.

I was a young Assistant Manager and one evening I was visiting the European Club in Sungai Lembing. Wilf was a soft-spoken Englishman somewhere in his fifties, and he worked in the Engineering Department of The Pahang Consolidated Company Limited tin mine. Part of his job was to inspect the narrow gauge railway network that was used for getting the tin down to Pasir Kemudi, where it was shipped in barges down the river to Kuantan. The railway was also used for logging and other transportation needs. However, the primary purpose of the railway was to transport the heavy, small picul-sized sacks of tin ore to the market in Singapore. The railway lines were laid on wooden sleepers sawn from logs adjacent to the carpentry shop at Sungai Lembing, situated

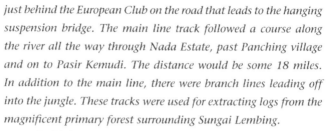

just behind the European Club on the road that leads to the hanging suspension bridge. The main line track followed a course along the river all the way through Nada Estate, past Panching village and on to Pasir Kemudi. The distance would be some 18 miles. In addition to the main line, there were branch lines leading off into the jungle. These tracks were used for extracting logs from the magnificent primary forest surrounding Sungai Lembing.

On his long-distance railway inspection rounds, Wilf drove a motorised four-wheel trolley. The mechanical engineers had utilised a small Ford car engine and modified it in order to propel the heavy, wooden-planked trolley along the railway line. When driving the trolley ,Wilf sat on a comfortable chair, with simple throttle and braking mechanisms within easy reach. He loved these trips. He was alone in untamed and beautiful jungle countryside; sometimes, the noise of the trolley would startle brilliantly-coloured birds to take off and fly ahead of him, or he would catch sight of wild pigs or even rusa deer. The forward movement of the trolley afforded a delightful cooling breeze, and he had rigged up a simple canvas awning as protection against the hot sun and the rain. Wilf always took with him some sandwiches, a thermos of tea and some water. As I recall, he had a West Country, or Cornish English accent.

"Well, there I was then, sittin' up on me trolley, footlin' along the line coming in to Nada. She was workin' a bit hard because there's a gradient just there, and a fairly sharpish right turn into a long cutting, very steep on both sides. I got to the top and she picked up speed and we fairly rushed into the cutting, and bless my soul if there wasn't a tiger in there, on the line, right in front of me, he was starin' me straight in the eyes. I hit the brakes, but it takes a bit of time to get the speed off that trolley. As I pulled on the brake for all I was worth I watched Mr Stripes leap for all *he was worth straight up the bank. But it was too steep for him, see, and he didn't make it, did he? Fell back, right down on top of me and knocked me off the trolley. I rolled down the side of the track into the drain. Well I picked myself up as sharp as I could and looked around to see what was happening. The trolley just kept on movin'. But, for an instant there was me, on one side of the trolley, and a very frightened tiger on the other. Well, I took off fast after the trolley. Fortunately Stripes took off in the other direction. I caught up the trolley when it finally stopped, and I poured myself a cup of tea."*

When pressed to say what frightened him most about the whole experience, Wilf said, "It was when I saw the soil right at the top of the cutting, giving way under his claws. It was like a film in slow motion. I saw him clawing at soil that was just breaking away and I thought to myself, I don't like this Wilf. I don't like it one bit."

CHAPTER 6

Working With George Wood

Maurice did say one thing to me, which I suppose could be considered as helpful advice. "George Wood is coming back next week. He's had his six months' leave, he'll be taking over from me." He paused and toyed with his chest hair. "So he is the man you have to get on with. Not me. I'm leaving. I'm retiring. George Wood is the man. He'll be your next manager." We were sitting in the Land Rover, driving up the steep hill from the Panching factory on the way to the office. Maurice kept the Land Rover in fourth gear until it was far too late to change, then rammed the gear stick forward into third gear. Having lost most of the engine's revs, and rather than attempt the change into 2nd gear, he rocked backwards and forwards in his seat. I think he was trying to help the vehicle up the hill, his foot clamped hard down on the accelerator pedal. "Now you remember what I tell you," shouted Maurice above the din of a labouring engine. "It's George Wood you have to get on with."

Unfortunately, I did not get on with George Wood. Perhaps it was wrong chemistry from the start. I am sure it was as much my fault as it was his. George is now retired from Planting, and even though he is a Scot, his Malaysian wife and him have chosen to live somewhere in England. George is one of those Scots that Englishmen often refer to 'professional Scots'. He was Scottish with an attitude that reflects the ancient, and not entirely misplaced dislike and mistrust some Scots have for the English. There is such a marked difference between so many of the Scots I have met. Some are arrogant, blustery and feign a clannish superiority. Some are cultured, pragmatic, and are great gentlemen. Today, I am of course aware of the atrocious treatment the Scots have suffered at the hands of the English. And from my travels, reading, meeting Scots and from listening to English and Scottish historians I now know how unforgivably brutal and full of shame is English history. The English have perpetrated atrocities and subjected the Scots to generations of deprivation that would, in today's political reality, call for international sanctions against the English.

George Wood seemed to carry all this antagonism with him. It was like a Scottish cloak slung over his shoulder, weighing him down in spite of his striding energy. George always struck me as a severe person. He was a stickler for doing the right thing at the right time; for never breaking his own personal laws of propriety. His severity was encapsulated in the way he would say, "No, no. I have to be getting along," whether it was staying for a cup of tea or for another whisky soda. His moody, locked-in silences also affected me, because, for some months, I was carried along on his tide and my life was played to his tune.

I think George genuinely found it difficult to talk to me. I was callow, young and English. George, therefore, in the pedantic way that is typical of certain Scots, lectured me. George constantly told me how things were. If I made a statement he would consider it for a few moments, then surgically cut my proposition to pieces. I am afraid this awoke something very obstinate and unpleasant in me. He was in his thirties, full of experience from the oil industry in Bahrain or Abu Dhabi, well educated and very disciplined— I was hopelessly young and fresh on the estate. He was my boss, and I had better not forget it.

Soon after George's arrival from his six months' leave in Scotland, he and I were transferred, away from the main division

Sungai Talam Estate; Maurice Cotterhill's retirement as Manager of Sungai Talam Rubber Estates Ltd, August 1958. Bottom row, left to right: the author is unable to recall the names of the first two men; Mr L. Thomas, conductor, Panching; Mr Mohammed Sidek (with spectacles), conductor and hospital dresser, Sungai Talam Estate; Mr K. Thomas, conductor, Nada Estate; Mr George, assistant clerk, head office; Mr M. Thomas, conductor of Sungai Talam Estate until author arrived; Mr Melvyn Gordon, Scottish Assistant Manager, Panching; Mr George Wood, Scottish Head Assistant previously in charge of Nada Estate; Mr Maurice Cotterill MBE, English Manager, Panching; Sybil Cotterill; Philippa Cotterill; Michael Thorp (author), English Assistant Manager, Sungai Talam; Mr C. Cherian, Chief Clerk, Panching; Mr K Chacko, hospital dresser, Panching; Mr Varghese, junior conductor, Panching, a Malay *mandor*, Panching; the Chinese school teacher, Panching; the author is unable to recall the name of the last person in the row. Other people in the picture are *mandors*, *kenganies*, drivers and contractors.

at Panching, to Sungai Talam Estate. I was under no illusion of the fact that it was George who was in charge. The idea was to teach me how to deal with check rolls and the day-to-day running of an estate, so that I was in a position to take over the supervision of Sungai Talam on my own, with the title of Assistant-in-Charge. When that goal was achieved, George was scheduled to go back up to Panching to concentrate on understudying Maurice before Maurice and Sybil left Malaya for good.

For almost three months, George and I had to share the Sungai Talam bungalow. The bungalow is now torn down and its very whereabouts forgotten. We shared every meal, the cost of food and housekeeping and almost every minute of the working day. I wish that George and I could have been friends, but in my opinion, he was far too much the boss. I do not think he ever considered us as being colleagues; I was his junior, his assistant, and that meant that I should know my place. It is strange and sad that we learn all too late in life that having a job and working well is all about people. It does not matter how clever or brilliant a person is, or how much he or she knows, if that person is unable to win the respect of his colleagues and achieve leadership by example rather than by fear. When employees fear their manager, it matters little how brilliant he may be, because that type of leadership closes off any type of initiative or creative approach from the employees, and certainly does not lead to success in business or in the management of rubber estates.

I had a poor teacher in George; he taught me arrogance in my attitude to the staff and the labour force. He addressed them as if they were commodities rather than people. It is so easy to be wise with hindsight; so simple to see what should have been done. To my credit, some of our differences were related to my objections to his supercilious and demeaning approach to the labour force. I remember on one particular occasion, when George's two boxer dogs attacked a miserable little local dog belonging to one of the labour force. The local dog, half the size of George's bitch, was screaming and gurgling as both of George's dogs bit and shook it to the point of death. I exploded, "Get your bloody dogs off George. They're going to kill that poor animal."

"They shouldn't have a dog with them in the field." came

George's laconic response. I kicked at the arse end of the big male boxer, which surprised the brute enough to make it let go its stranglehold on the other dog. George then grabbed his own bitch by a back leg and pulled her away. In the respite, the local dog made off towards the labour lines, pathetically dragging its back legs.

"Don't you ever kick my dog again," George hissed at me, his mouth twitching in anger. It was not his style to shout. But he was trembling with rage.

"If that had been my dog," I said, pointing in the direction of the retreating animal, "I would have been into your dogs with a *changkul*." I'm afraid my fate was sealed.

Eventually, George handed over Sungai Talam Estate to me, loaded his belongings in his Land Rover and drove off. For the first time since my arrival I was living and working alone, that is, without the benefit of other British staff. Just prior to celebrating my 21st birthday, I was officially Assistant-in-Charge of Sungai Talam Estate. Situated some seven miles from Kuantan; close to the Bukit Goh forest reserve the Estate still had an elephant problem, the occasional tiger wandered through and there were plenty of wild pigs.

Being an expatriate, and employed by the Chairman in London, I was part of the total injustice of the British estate management system. From the point of view of the senior Asian staff of the Kuala Reman Rubber Estates, I had been dumped on Sungai Talam Estate right in front of the nose of yet another Mr Thomas. He was also a Malayali Indian, in his late-thirties, married, and at that time he and his wife had one son, Surish. Mr Thomas had effectively managed the division for well over a year before I arrived. Imagine the chagrin he felt when a twenty one-year-old English lout was quite arbitrarily dropped on him, and, technically he, the man who had been efficiently running things, was no longer in charge; he had lost his authority.

Had he wished, Mr Thomas could have totally withdrawn his support and allowed me to sink in a mire of my own making without my realising what was happening. But he did not. Instead, he chose to teach me my job, counsel me, and to put me right in a gentle but unmistakeably firm manner. He was a wonderful man. And I am sorry to say that I took him for granted. However, during a recent visit to Kuantan, I met him after a church service at The Anglican Church, The Church of the Epiphany. "Do you remember me?" I asked, springing a gap of more than forty years on him. He looked at me, the peculiar white fleck he had in his left eye as memorable, as if he was staring at me across the office table 40 years previously. "No," he said. "I do not remember you."

"Sungai Talam Estate," I said. "You had a house next to the multiplication nursery, by the divisional office. You have a son called Surish." For a moment, a terrible thought flashed into my mind. What if he remembers me with distaste? What if I conjure up some bad memories for him? After all, I stretch back into colonial times in Malaya. He was now part of a thriving dynamic and thrusting country that had long since thrown off its colonial shadow. I wondered if when he recognised me he might turn on his heel and walk away. Fortunately he did not. Thomas is a gentleman in the true sense of the word. He acknowledged me in a kindly manner, but I could tell that our meeting had triggered off a host of memories in him, and they were all racing through his mind.

"Mr Thomas," I said, shaking his hand. "You taught me my job. Thank you." I should have said to him, what I say to him now: Thomas, certain people influence our lives, some in a good way and some in an unhappy way. You have been a good influence in my life. You taught me much more than my job. You taught me by example what wisdom, patience and respect can achieve. These lessons you unconsciously passed on to me; though they have taken a lifetime to sink in, I recognise where they have come from and that makes me smile, and I also thank you for that.

CHAPTER 7

Loneliness Can Lead In Many Directions

I have approached this chapter in my life so many times, and so many times, I have turned away. I suppose there is in all people, the dark, hidden side; that part of our personality we do not show to others. I have thought of writing this chapter many times, and I question why I should write it, and at the same time I ask myself why am I so reluctant?

When George Wood and I were transferred to Sungai Talam Estate, early in 1957, we took over the Sungai Talam Estate bungalow from the Manager of Atbara Estate, Brian Gahan. The Atbara manager's bungalow had, until approximately 1954, been situated on the northern side of the Sungai Lembing road, but it was burnt to the ground by Communist terrorists. For just over two years, Gahan had rented the Sungai Talam manager's bungalow from Kuala Reman Rubber Estates. When George and I moved to Sungai Talam, Atbara Estate had recently been sold local Malaysian Chinese interests. The Chinese proprietors decided there was no longer a need for a European Manager on Atbara, so Gahan was to proceed to South Africa on leave, and if he returned to Malaya, he would eventually be transferred to another estate within his agency. It was agreed that George and I would give employment to the two Chinese girls who had been running the bungalow for Gahan as well as cooking his food and doing the washing.

Gahan did not join in the general European run of things in Kuantan. He was a loner. People said of him, as if to explain his behaviour, that he had been incarcerated in Changi gaol by the Japanese during the 2nd World War. He was not a member of the Kuantan Club. This in itself was enough to send a strong message of not wanting too much to do with the British establishment. He left Kuantan sometime before Merdeka in 1957. I hardly knew him. Today I think of him, as I am tempted to think of so many other British planters who spent some years as managers of rubber estates. How they would weep if they knew that their life's work was now given over to a golf club, low-cost housing and factories, The terraces that were created on the hills for rubber trees, and the drains that were constructed in the low-lying areas have now been flattened and filled by bulldozers.

Sungai Talam Estate bungalow, 1957. It has since been demolished.

In the case of Atbara Esate, it is now a luxurious golf course and country club, and the most prominent piece of high ground has become the residence of The Tengku Mahkota of Pahang, a glistening blue-tiled palace somewhere close to the site where the Communist terrorists torched the Manager's bungalow. At the time, when Gahan was in charge of the Estate, elephants roamed through Atbara, leaving their droppings along the Estate roads. The Communist terrorists used the field roads through Atbara as an escape route to reach the Bukit Goh forest reserve and the protection of the jungle. Today, there are enormous college buildings and the highway to Kuala Lumpur clips its edge.

When George Wood left Sungai Talam and I was to live alone in the bungalow it was agreed that I could not afford to employ the two Chinese girls. Only one of them was willing to stay on and work with me, while the other was not so keen. Through an interpreter, the girl who wanted to leave explained that the reason was because she had an opportunity to go back to tapping rubber and she would like the change. I remember thinking, even then, how thoughtful and sensitive of her to explain that she had valid reasons for not wanting to work for me rather than leave me with the opposite impression. It was a combination of Chinese pragmatism and not wanting to burn any boats as well as sensitivity for my feelings. So she left to become a tapper on Atbara Estate, and Ah Moi stayed to work for me as my cook and wash *amah*, becoming part of my life.

The tiger that took the dog at Sungai Talam

One afternoon I had a visit from J and Edna Windsor. They called in to Sungai Talam Esate to invite me that evening for potluck, as Edna delighted in calling her cooking. I invited them to join me for tea. We sat upstairs in the front of the bungalow with its beautifully polished floor and J revealed that when he was a very young man, he had lived on Sungai Talam. J explained that it was at the time, about 1908, when the original jungle was cleared to make way for the rubber trees that comprised Sungai Talam Estate. He was touched, and a little amused to think that the trees he had originally been responsible for were now being cleared and replanted under my supervision.

"Of course I never lived in this bungalow. There was a different bungalow in those days," he explained. "It was further down the hill, close to where your kerani's *house is today." He took a long pull at his pipe before continuing. "There was still a lot of jungle around the bungalow, it was a single story affair with an attap roof." He took his pipe out of his mouth and tapped some ash and tobacco into the ashtray. "Well, we did not have diesel generators for electricity in those days. So, if you wanted to read, it was a paraffin lamp and you would strain your vision, and try to keep all the flying ants and bugs out of your hair." His merry eyes looked at me, as if to challenge the easy existence I had in comparison. "I used to save my serious reading until the evening, when I went to bed," he continued. "I used to tuck the mosquito net in all round the mattress and have the oil lamp on the outside of the net on the bedside table. I got the light but not the bugs." He paused again, his blue eyes staring out across the canopy of rubber trees. "I remember one night, when the whole damn mosquito net caught fire. I was out of that bed pretty quickly, I can tell you."*

When Ah Moi had served the tea and some buttered Jacob's Cream crackers J felt the need to continue his story. Usually he was a quiet man, quite content to listen to his wife, Edna, do the talking. "I was sitting on my veranda reading a newspaper, and the dog was sitting by the side of my chair. He looked out at the final rays of the setting sun. "It was about now, well perhaps a little later in the evening. I remember the sun had only just gone, but it was still light." He took a sip of his tea and leaned back in his chair, his story apparently ended.

"Well," Edna said, with her proprietary smile. She quite obviously loved J and humoured him, and played along with his little foibles, but sometimes found the suspense of going along with his stories too much to bear. "Aren't you going to tell Michael what happened?" she

demanded. She had obviously heard the story before.

"Well, he took the dog didn't he? J's eyes sparkled mischievously with the pleasure of knowing that he had us both on the edge of our chairs. "The tiger was suddenly there, beside me with a bang, it brushed against my newspaper and seized the dog before the poor thing had a chance to get up on all fours, and then it was off—straight over the side of the veranda wall. It was all over in a second," said J. "Well of course, I was almost at ground level in that bungalow and the tiger must have been sniffing around for days. We had seen his pug marks, so I knew he was around somewhere."

"Did you have a gun?" I asked in shocked amazement.

"It was leaning up against the wall, a rifle. No more that two feet away from me, didn't get a chance." J put his cup and saucer down on the circular glass-topped rattan table. "When I had picked up the gun and stood looking out over the veranda wall, all I saw was movement in the sedge grass which showed where he had gone." He thought for a couple of seconds, and then added, "He was fast." He smiled and said, "He was fast alright, fast and hungry."

All three of us sat quietly for a few seconds thinking our own thoughts. Mine, I must admit, were pursuing the possibility of a repeat performance by a tiger on my own dog. He slept downstairs without being tied in an open box kennel that did not offer much protection. J relit his pipe. "The pity was," he said. "It was a damn good dog."

J and Edna are both buried in Kuantan, in the cemetery at Tanjong Api. Edna was left a widow, without children and she spent her last years in a chalet on the beach at Telok Cempedak. She was born on 18th January 1905 and she died in Kuantan, 18th April 1993. The two of them, Edna and J, participants in so much of the history of Pahang, rest in separate graves. Not, I think, from choice, but because the policy of those in charge of the cemetery is not to open a grave for a second burial.

CHAPTER 8

Maurice In The Jungle And On Merdeka Day

Maurice was a very special man. I joined Kuala Reman Estate at a time when he was seemingly very much looking forward to his retirement. At the age of fifty-five, he was entitled to his planters' Provident Fund (PPF) retirement benefits. As far as I can recall, like most Planters at that time, the Planter who was member of the PPF scheme was deducted an amount of 5 per cent of his basic emoluments, and the company paid-in twice as much to the fund or 10 per cent into the planter's account. This combined total was entered to the benefit of the planter as a pension in the form of a capital accumulation and he was entitled to receive the full amount after 10 years of service. If a planter left the industry prior to having served 10 years, then he was only entitled to his own, lesser contribution. It was yet another discreet and subtle way in which the employers bound their expatriate employees in a tempting web of reward.

Maurice was special in one remarkable way. When the Japanese occupation forces arrived in Malaya they travelled down the East Coast with very little organised military opposition from local or The Combined Commonwealth Military Forces. The Japanese reached Kuantan and hurried up the road to Sungai Lembing to secure the tin mine. Maurice Cotterill and three other Europeans, Tyson and Vincent Baker and his sister Nona Baker, decided that they would have a better chance of resisting capture if they disappeared into the jungle and avoided the Japanese. Some of these events are described in Spencer Chapman's book

The Jungle is Neutral and also *Paai Naa*, a book written about Nona Baker by Dorothy Thatcher and Robert Cross. It is a fascinating account of Nona Baker, concerning her experiences when she moved to Sungai Lembing to become housekeeper for her brother in the years leading up to the Japanese invasion.

Nona Baker's story begins with events from the time that Vincent Baker started work at the tin mine in Sungai Lembing in 1911. By 1930, the community under his control numbered more than 8,000 and he was one of two Europeans who were unofficial members of the Pahang State Council. The main story of the book, however, is concerned with the events leading up to the Japanese invasion and how they endured incarceration in the jungle, free of the Japanese, but dependent on the local Chinese who were in the process of building up a Communist insurgency force bent on ridding Malaya of the Japanese and equally intent on not allowing the British to resume power.

The Japanese arrived in Sungai Lembing on 3rd March 1942. Nona Baker's story continues, and she describes how, with the help of very brave local Chinese employees Cheng Kam, Wong Ng and Lau Siu, the Bakers were housed and fed on the edge of a jungle clearing quite close to Sungai Lembing. As the danger of their discovery by the Japanese increased, the Bakers were moved several times. Eventually they joined the Communist Forces at a camp near Batu Sawah under the control of Lao Chung and Lao Lee.

Nona Baker survived until the Japanese surrendered in 1945. Her brother, Vincent Baker, powerful General Manager of the PCCL tin-mine, died in the jungle a broken man.

There is a paragraph about food. Nona Baker informs her biographers:

"There was not an animal or reptile that did not find its way into the pot. Lizards have a delicate flavour and their unhatched eggs are delicious; young crocodiles are not unpleasant and when chopped into smaller bits could pass as snails. Python tastes like chicken provided it is skinned alive and eaten fresh. Boar, deer of all kinds, wild buffalo taste excellent." The quotation continues, and Nona Baker repeats her understanding of the Chinese belief concerning available food: "Monkey's brains if eaten warm with life bestow wisdom. The genitals of a bear confer immortality on the consumer."

It is possible that these four European expatriates, three men and one woman, considered that the Japanese invasion of Malaya would only be short-lived. They no doubt consoled themselves with the thought that the British, Australian and Indian Forces would soon have the Japanese cleared out of peninsular Malaya and Singapore. Tyson suffered from sugar diabetes. He depended on insulin treatment to hold his blood sugar levels in check." I am not sure how long he lasted in the jungle, but he died and Cotterill buried him. According to what Maurice told me, Tyson's end was hastened because he developed a blood poisoning as a result of infected leech bites.

Leeches are a problem for Planters, but we get to know how to deal with them. It is important to constantly watch for them, particularly in the jungle or in *belukar*. One has to examine the legs, the arms, the face and the neck; indeed, any part of the anatomy that comes into contact with leaves and branches. The body search, simply involves stopping somewhere where the light is good and checking to see if a leech has fastened itself or is in the process of looking for a soft spot. If you find one, it is best to try to ball it up between your thumb and forefinger before it gets a chance to bite through the skin and start the process of absorbing blood. Leech bites itch, sometimes maddeningly, particularly if the leech is knocked off and a tiny particle of its sucker arrangements is left in the wound. The important thing is to not scratch, even more so with dirty fingers and fingernails, because there is a very good chance of the bites becoming infected and turning into ulcerous sores or even getting maggoty from fly visitations.

I do not know how long Tyson lasted from the time that he and the others decided to retreat into the jungle. However, he and Cotterill were at some stage instructed by the Communists on whom they had come to depend, to travel from Pahang all the way to Johore for some strategic reason. It is probable that Tyson died sometime shortly after the completion of that journey. It must be the best part of 200 kilometers and the trip was probably made at night, with little food, keeping to the jungle or to isolated estate roads to avoid detection.

Maurice survived in the jungle for the entire period of the Japanese occupation, a period of more than three years. At one juncture he was contacted by Spencer Chapman of Force 136 fame. Chapman was parachuted into Malaya in order to find out as much as he could for the British in regard to recapturing Malaya from the Japanese. Chapman invited Maurice to participate in sabotage raids. I think Maurice declined on the grounds that if he continued to be anonymous, the Japanese, although they most certainly knew he was in the jungle, would not bother to utilise important resources in order to try to capture him. On the other hand, if he were to start blowing up bridges and ambushing Japanese troops he would represent a threat the Japanese would be forced to do something about. According to his book, Chapman seemed disappointed in Maurice's lack of patriotic zeal. According to Maurice, the whole episode was about survival.

However, in 1957, not long before Maurice left the country

for good, I was invited to spend a weekend together with Maurice and his wife, Sybil. They also invited George Wood and the two other British assistants, Melvin Gordon and Alan Martin. Maurice summoned all three of us, his British staff, to the bungalow for a Saturday pre-lunchtime drink. Under Sybil's watchful eye Maurice poured out large glasses of cold Anchor beer, which he no doubt had obtained duty-free from the concession godown in Sungai Lembing.

I must tell an endearing story about Maurice. However, at the outset I must explain that he certainly was not mean. Sybil kept a careful check on his drinking and a beady eye on the amount of beer he consumed, as it did not take more than a few glasses to make him loud of voice, but generally difficult to understand. When he was drunk, Maurice had difficulty in forming words into sentences and, in his cups, he spent a lot of time tugging his chest hair and trying to focus on what was going on around him. But he loved his beer.

Maurice was well aware that Sybil kept an eye on things. When he poured out beer for his guests that Saturday lunchtime he poured rapidly so that we were handed glasses of froth that soon settled to less than half a glass, which, of course, was soon emptied. Maurice poured his own beer carefully down the side of a tilted glass so that he ended up with a full glass. Naturally, no host would allow his guests to sit with an empty glass in their hands so Maurice jumped up at frequent intervals to fill our glasses, indeed as often as necessary. This gave him the chance to empty his glass and get a refill. Sybil, in her inimitable way and with fluttering eyelids murmured a quiet word of caution to her husband, "Maurice!" He flashed his crooked smile and said, "No, no, my dear. It's not me it's these assistants of mine they are all such thirsty young men."

During that session we, were discussing amongst ourselves what equipment we would take with us, if we were faced with the necessity to do what Maurice had done when he fled the Japanese and disappeared into the jungle. We made lists as long as our arms and covered everything from a *parang*, the large useful knife that could help slash a path, toothpaste, anti-malarial medicine, vitamin tablets, tins of food, sacks of rice, cooking utensils, radios, batteries and all sorts of suggestions including tobacco and bottles of whisky. Maurice simply laughed. Try as we may, we were unable to draw him out and get him to share his experiences. He did not talk about those years in the jungle; he pushed them away. However, it was a fact that he had spent a lot of time together with the Chinese Communist resistance groups who were interested in tossing the Japanese out of Malaya and ensuring that the British never came back. Their goal was to establish a Communist puppet regime, supported by and paying allegiance to Peking.

For much of the time Maurice spent in the jungle he lived with, and cooked for, the groups of Chinese who later became terrorists. Maurice knew many of these men and must have known something of their background, whether they were teachers or bus drivers or clerks in banks and insurance companies. For more than three years, Maurice enjoyed the security that many different camps afforded him. In return he cooked, made himself useful and, in all probability, kept his mouth shut. His knowledge of the communist supporters, who later became terrorists during the Emergency (1948–1962), and the fact that he had shared campsites with them in the jungle, could possibly have been the reason why he came unscathed through the Emergency. The communists must have known where Maurice was; they must have been able to shoot him on many occasions, they knew that he had taken over Kuala Reman Rubber Estates after the ambush and slaughter of Jennings, Rutty and the Chinese dresser in 1948. They just left him alone

There is one incident I should relate. I feel very sure that I have heard this story from Maurice himself. In my mind, I seem to recall that Maurice told the story to me and a visitor to the estate, perhaps a Visiting Agent or a man called Linton, a Scot, and the Thomas Cowan white ant building inspector. He told us the story when we were seated in the upstairs lounge in the old Manager's bungalow at Panching. However, I am unable to remember just how we got into the conversation, and, indeed, how we managed to get Maurice to talk about it at all. Maurice told us that on more than one occasion, his Chinese comrades, when they had been out of the jungle on some sort of mission, brought back with them into the camp a heart or liver cut out of the chest of one of their killed or captured Japanese army officers. The Chinese, he told us, ate these body parts and Maurice said that he was invited to partake. But he said he never did. At the time I accepted this as a fact. It would not have entered into my head to question the truth of his reply. Today, as I write about the incident I find myself wondering if the price of his admission to the jungle camps, part of the cost of being afforded shelter with the Chinese; to be a non-card carrying part of their group, was to join in the ritual of eating the heart of a sworn enemy and oppressor. To not accept their invitation could have involved him in a far worse plight than simply swallowing a morsel of human flesh.

Maurice was appointed Manager of Kuala Reman Estate in 1948, shortly after the previous Manager, Jennings and his Assistant Rutty were murdered in an ambush near Pasir Kemudi. The bodies of the two Europeans were hacked and mutilated. The body of the Chinese hospital assistant, who was obviously killed by the Communists in error, was covered and protected from the rays of the sun and marauding flies. He was properly laid out with respect and honour for the dead. Both Europeans, although Rutty was from New Zealand, are buried in the Tanjong Api Christian cemetery in Kuantan, close to the point where the river meets the sea. Their tombstones are still in good condition although the names are starting to weather and fade. These graves represent a period of relatively modern Pahang history, a past that very few modern Malaysians know about today. One is tempted to ask: why should young Malaysians know about this, why should they care about the graves of two Europeans? The men buried in that cemetery were part of the colonial period. Jennings and Rutty were both planters and they were killed by communist terrorists. Terrorists who, with the passage of time, may come to be regarded as patriots, as it could be said that the communists assisted in some measure to hasten the process of independence from the British. Their nuisance values, and the cost in terms of money and British lives accelerated the independence hand-over negotiations. Those tombstones are history.

The nine years that Maurice was Manager of Kuala Reman Rubber Estates, from 1948 until he retired in 1957, were difficult to say the least. Communist terrorist activity made living on an estate a harrowing experience for the Manager and his assistants, as well as for the staff and the labour force. Maurice however, survived and was also awarded the M.B.E. in recognition of his very special services to the British nation and for his fortitude in the jungle during the war.

One thing I learnt during my stay in Panching was that all the field staff and the *kanganies* very carefully observed the manner in which Maurice carried his walking stick when he was out on his inspection rounds on the Estate. If he whacked at flowers and weeds with the end of his stick as he walked, then it would be a good idea to simply turn off the main road and head into the rubber, avoiding him at all costs. If he was swinging his stick and using it like a walking stick, even though he had absolutely no need, then, that too, would be a good occasion to try to avoid him. However, if he was carrying the stick in the middle, or had it tucked under his arm, Sergeant Major-style, then you could hold your course and even risk calling out "*Selamat pagi*". It was said that if he had the stick across his shoulders and he was hanging or resting his arms on the stick, then, that was a particularly auspicious time, and it was a good idea if you wanted to request a day's leave, to ask him there and then.

Just prior to his retirement, Maurice sent word that he wanted to meet me on Sungai Talam Estate at 7:00 am at the western entrance in Field 8. The message was passed on to me by Mr Ho Sek Wan, who was the Pahang Consolidated Company Limited's secretary based in Kuantan. He was a great gentleman, employed for years by the company as forwarding and receiving agent, generally doing everything he could for the tin mining company in Sungai Lembing. When I had shipments of rubber from Sungai Talam they were sent into Kuantan to the PCCL godown on the bank of the Kuantan River, where Sek Wan took care of all the shipment details. He was also a good friend, and, through the years, I was the grateful recipient of much advice and carefully thought out suggestions from him.

Early the following morning, I took a lift on the estate lorry with Haroun, the driver to Field 8. As the lorry ground its gears and disappeared back up the hill, I waited for Maurice to appear. It was an indescribably beautiful morning and at 6:45 am at Field 8, where I was clean-shaven and wearing my newly scrubbed

Bata field boots, the gibbons in the Bukit Goh forest reserve, a few miles away, joined in my celebration of the morning by their unmistakeable and sad howling. I was early on purpose, as to be late would have been an unthinkable disaster, and Maurice was perfectly capable of turning up ahead of time and striding off without me. I had, on more than one occasion, chased after him around the estate lamely asking tappers or other workers I met if they had seen the *tuan besar*. On those occasions I swear he had arrived in advance of the agreed time. However, on this particular morning I turned up at Field 8 a quarter of an hour early, giving me enough time to compose myself, and in my mind, run through yield figures and labour force details which I had scribbled on a note in my pocket.

At 6:55 am, the green, canvas hooded Land Rover appeared round the bend in the road coming from the direction of Panching. Maurice, who always seemed angry, climbed out of the vehicle and impatiently explained to the driver that he should come back to the Sungai Talam Esate office at 9:30 am to pick him up. This was good news for me, as it would mean that I probably did not have to suffer through the ordeal of giving Maurice breakfast. It was not the eating part that was difficult, nor the business of asking Ah Moi to prepare some toast and fried eggs. It was the awful minefield of having to make conversation with him, of not knowing his mood, and then, if I asked the wrong question, having to endure one of his lashing silences.

He grunted "Good morning" and we set off. We traversed the whole of the Field 8 boundary between the estate and a strip of jungle on a *lalang* search. To my enormous relief, we did not find a single blade of the grass, *imperata cylindrical*, an insidious weed that is sprayed, forked or wiped with oil in constant efforts to keep it out of the estate. I continued to follow Maurice, who was never one to walk around difficult terrain, and we slid and dropped down a steep gully onto a field road where he decided to ask a few questions. "How are the yields in Field 6?" He grunted. "Is the stimulant having an effect?"

"Yes sir," I replied, walking very fast to keep up with him.

"What about pre-coagulation, any sign of that?" He barked. I was delighted. It was just the right question, because during the time immediately after muster and meeting Maurice that very morning, I had quizzed Mr Sidek, our Malay conductor responsible for tapping, on just how one would deal with pre-coagulation. Sidek had explained to me that particular attention to knife, bucket and cup hygiene or general cleanliness was essential, and the judicial and careful use of a sodium sulphite solution that should be poured into the cups at the time of tapping.

"We have had a small problem," I cheerfully replied.

"Well," said Maurice, continuing to press ahead at his usual pace. "How do you deal with that?"

"We are paying particular care with regard to hygiene." I said, in what must have been an irritating tone of voice. "We are checking buckets prior to collection and not allowing any collection from the cups if there are any signs of residual latex from the day before."

"Residual latex?" repeated Maurice. "What the hell's that?"

"Dirty cups and buckets, sir. Insufficiently cleaned."

"Exactly. Why don't you speak English? Residual latex, indeed."

"And," I continued, not yet having learnt that to preempt Maurice Cotterill and certain Visiting Agents was fatal, "we have been using sodium sulphite in the cup." I really felt quite chuffed with myself. I felt quite the Planter.

"What solution of sodium sulphite have you been using?"

Maurice asked, slowing his pace slightly, in order to more fully experience the full flavour of my reply. "What dilution have you been using?" Of course, I did not have the answer in my head. It was written in my notebook, but to whip it out of my pocket in the middle of field rounds was not a good idea. And, of course, I was too unknowing and callow and green to keep my mouth shut—or better still, confess that I did not know.

"Er, I think it's about 10 per cent, sir. Yes. Yes, it's 10 per cent." Maurice stopped walking altogether and whacked at some innocent flowery heads with his stick. He turned round to look me full in the face.

"Where did you get that information?" he asked. His blue eyes had turned steely grey, and his voice had that edge of chalk on a blackboard that warned me to be careful.

"It was Mr Sidek. In fact I asked him just this morning."

"And he told you 10 per cent?" It was quietly, carefully worded—but in a tone I knew was loaded with all sorts of dangers.

"I'm not sure of the percentage, sir." I chose not to look at him when I owned up.

"But just now you were quite sure," he said, and swung round on his heel away from me and started walking at his usual brisk pace. It was a Maurice demonstration, yet another manifestation of his impatience with his European assistants. He said nothing more to me during the rest of the field round until a couple of hours later, when we arrived at the packing shed. This silence, intended as a moody punishment, was the measure of Maurice's capacity to play cat and mouse. He knew that his silence would give me time to reflect on all my shortcomings. It gave him time to savour my discomfort and demonstrate his contempt for the young planters who were in his charge. When we stepped into the packing shed, into the rich smell of ribbed smoked sheet and the cheap scent the female sorters used, Mr Sidek left his desk and walked over to the entrance to respectfully greet Maurice.

"Mr Sidek," Maurice addressed the Malay conductor with considerably more warmth in his voice than he used to address me. "Mr Thorp seems to think that we should use a 10 per cent solution of sodium sulphite in the bottles issued to the tappers, for sprinkling in the cup at the time of tapping. What do you say?" Sidek listened to the question with polite, but not obsequious attention. The seconds ticked by and Sidek looked intensely into Maurice's face. I thought for a moment that Sidek had not understood the question. However, Sidek thoughtfully looked in my direction and I could tell that he had immediately sensed that I was in hot water. Sidek continued to look thoughtful for a few seconds, and, when the pause had reached the point where he could no longer delay giving an answer he said, "In the bottles, Sir, it would be point zero five per cent." Then, again flicking a careful glance at me he went on, "I expect Mr Thorp was thinking of the stock solution we make in the early morning, when we mix 1 pound of sodium sulphite with 3 gallons of water." Mr Sidek saved my hide. At the same time, he gave me a lesson in being loyal to colleagues that I hope I shall never forget.

I invited Maurice back to the bungalow for breakfast, but he requested only a drink of squash or a glass of boiled and filtered water. When we walked from the office up towards the bungalow we passed the lorry, a fairly new Bedford 5-ton truck, with the words KUALA REMAN RUBBER ESTATES proudly painted in black along the grey sides of the body. It was parked in its shed beside Mr Thomas' house. Maurice stopped for a few moments and stared at the lorry. "I shall not be here on 31st August, on Merdeka Day." He proclaimed. "I mean, I shall not come down

Dungun, East Coast, West Malaysia, 1959. Giant turtle covering her eggs before returning to the sea. From left to right: Bill Dishington, Manager, Mercantile Bank, Kuantan and Michael Thorp (author).

to Kuantan. I shall stay up at Panching, just in case something happens." He continued to walk up towards my bungalow, and in a quieter, almost conspiratorial voice he said, "On Merdeka Day I want you to take the lorry and park it inside the security fence around your bungalow." He pointed to the bungalow entrance. "I think it best to park the lorry in the porch where you can keep an eye on it. I mean you never know. They may get excited and carried away at the idea of being independent. And they may want to take it out on us." He stopped and looked at me with a serious but somehow caring expression on his face that quite warmed me. "I don't know," he continued. "I mean I haven't heard anything, but you never know." The thought flashed through my mind that it would be foolhardy and somehow provocative to move the lorry away from its usual overnight parking. I had absolutely no form of weapon, not even a pistol for self-defence. I fancied that my walking stick would not take me far, if certain members of the Sungai Talam labour force took it into their heads to burn the lorry and beat my brains out in celebration of independence. I listened carefully to Maurice's instructions but I was also careful not to nod in agreement.

Merdeka celebrations went off beautifully. My labour force at Sungai Talam made quite a lot of noise. When writing the phrase 'my labour force', I realise just how paternal, colonial, patronising, demeaning and objectionable that phrase must sound today. But that is the way things were in the planting industry before independence. At Sungai Talam, at that time, they were indeed, 'my labour force.' Cheong Ming, the shop owner at Sungai Talam and an estate contractor, had rigged up loudspeakers linked to the radio. From about 10:00 pm that night, the Malay radio station boomed out across the football field, and the sound of happy commentary, Malay, Chinese and Indian music floated up past the multiplication nursery to the bungalow. The tiny Mariammah temple had a dozen oil lamps burning, and there were scores of National and State flags decorating the shop and the office. The historic events taking place in the capital city of Kuala Lumpur were broadcast to the Nation.

The loudspeakers continued to blare out until past midnight, relaying events at the handing over of power ceremony and describing the final pulling down and removal of the British flag and the hoisting of the Malayan flag to rousing cries of: "*Merdeka! Merdeka! Merdeka!*" We listened to the proud voice of Tengu Abdul Rahman booming out by radio to *kampungs* and villages throughout the nation, and the melody and words of the new national anthem

'*Negara-ku*', movingly achieving also a place in my heart.

During that long night of celebration, I thought it wise to quietly retire to my bungalow and not be seen. I at least heeded to some extent Cotterill's admonition for caution. Besides which, there was no wisdom in joining my own labourers in celebration. An unguarded remark, an understandable shout of defiance may have sparked off a foolish reaction. In any event, as part of the Empire, and influenced by my Planter peers, I felt that it was a sad time. From my blinkered and prejudiced point of view it was possible to imagine that independence from Britain, after so many years, was perhaps ill-judged, a foolhardy move by Malaya's politicians. Even the well-informed Europeans with a background in Malaya could be heard to say, "Imagine the audacity, the adventurous rashness of Malaya's leaders in pulling the country away from Britain, away from law and order and fair play." The very real British fear and the fear among Planters was that the country could topple backwards into corruption and mismanagement, an easy prey for Communism or despotism.

It is understandable that the British who were serving in Malaya and trained in the love of Empire, which was steeped in the tradition of the 'glory' of Britain, imbued with the rightness, the correctness of having colonies with the attendant obligation of demonstrating values and integrity, would feel some misgivings at the very idea of *merdeka*. Freedom from what? We were not such terribly bad masters, not so tyrannical, nowhere near as bad as the Dutch, or the Germans, or even the commercially adept Danes. After all, had we not been responsible for infrastructure development; the railway, hospitals, schools, roads, telecommunications? Didn't we leave a prosperous country behind us? Had we not introduced the Employees Provident Fund (EPF)? Did not Malaya, as it then was, choose to retain links with

Britain and the other Commonwealth countries? But of course, with hand on heart, that development only took place to facilitate even greater commercial colonial development. Development restricted to British or other friendly and reciprocating interests.

One of the entrenched myths of the British, as colonial masters, was to prattle on about integrity. "We are here for our integrity". Integrity! It was a word that was frequently trotted out and bandied around during my years of service in Malaya and eventually, Malaysia. However, upon serious reflection of the way in which we Europeans lived our day-to-day lives, integrity was not always part of our actual code of practice. We paid lip service to the virtue embodied in the word and resisted open bribes; but our way of living was, in essence, the very antipathy of integrity, that colonial buzz word we so pompously lorded about us with the ease of those who never really understand the true meaning of the concept.

As the historic and unique events of the evening unfolded, I listened to the English radio broadcast from Kuala Lumpur. Radio reception was punctuated by the noise of crackling static punctuating the commentary on the medium wave. It was independence for Malaya, tearing itself away from British colonial rule of some hundred and fifty years. It was 31st August, 1957. I sat in my bungalow, in the tenuous light of an oil lamp, slightly apprehensive, in case the population of Sungai Talam estate should take it into its collective head to bump off the young *tuan*. But eventually I slept. And the lorry slept quite peacefully in its accustomed place next to Mr Thomas' house.

A pye-dog enters my life

One morning at muster, one of those mornings when the threat of rain was in the air, a morning when we agonised over the decision as to

whether or not we should send out the tappers, I kicked or stumbled over
something. Something soft that I instinctively knew was an animal.
I thought it was a rat that somehow had got between my feet. I took a
frightened step backwards and flashed the beam of my torch down on
the ground, my guts knotting with that sudden prickling of alarm rats,
snakes and similar animals provoke in us. On the ground at my feet
was a puppy. I could see he was almost black with traces of brindle.
It was a male. His eyes were hardly open, he was unbelievably helpless.
I had kicked him over onto his back and he was struggling to regain his
feet. Even then I could see he was feisty, and tough, and full of the will
to live. In all probability, one of the Chinese tappers had picked him up
and brought him out to the Estate on the back of the lorry. I have never
found out, but I expect they picked him up somewhere, a kampung
perhaps, Ayer Puteh, even Kuantan. Picked him up and put him on the
back of the lorry. When they arrived at Sungai Talam they must have
set him down on the ground as muster was being called. That way,
the puppy was given a chance. The bitch, his mother, was relieved of a
mouth to feed. The house where he came from was relieved of the burden
of another litter of puppies. And he dropped into my life.

I took him home to my bungalow and put him in a box with sides
too high for him to climb out. He whimpered but settled down in the
comfort of an old "Good Morning" towel. I found some milk powder
downstairs in the kerosene fridge and mixed it with some of my hot
thermos coffee water so that it was warm, and I set it in front of him
in a saucer, and he went mad. He stood in it, and he upset the saucer
but he drank in a way that told me he would survive, that he had a
tremendous appetite for food and a strong will for life.

When I came back to the bungalow from my field rounds the rain
was pouring down. The Chinese tappers from Kuantan were still waiting
for transport home. However, I was mildly pleased that I had delayed
the decision to send them out to their tasks, as, according to the system

of those days, not sending them out to tap meant that I had saved the company a day's wages. It was an unfortunate decision for the tappers because they would receive nothing for all the hours they had spent by the temple waiting for our orders. If we had sent them out, and it rained while they were tapping, almost all the latex would be lost in the rain and the estate would have to pay for a washout. By delaying the decision we avoided making any payment. Bad for the tappers but good for my production figure costs.

When I returned to the bungalow it was raining hard but it was now full daylight so I examined the puppy I had been foolish enough to take into my life. Picking him up out of his box, I discovered he was crawling with lice and bugs. I found some insect powder and gave him a good rub. I left him sneezing and wrapped up in a towel full of powder, then after some minutes, to give the insecticide time to take effect, I gave him a warm bath. Dead bugs floated away from him on the surface of the water. I towelled him off and tried him with some more milk. He drank until I had to pull him away from the dish. I bundled him in to lots of dry towels and put him back in his box.

From then on it was really Ah Moi who looked after him. She nursed him, fed him and cared for him. He developed a special relationship with her. She talked to him, played with him, stroked him and mothered him. His attitude towards me was very different. He easily, and in good dog fashion, acknowledged me somehow as his rightful master. We were great friends, and, eventually, we became inseparable and I certainly think that on at least one occasion he may have saved my life. I called him Barney and he stayed with me for twelve years. When I left Malaysia, and as he was nearly thirteen years old I did not trust leaving him with anyone, I had to have him put down, as we euphemistically refer to destroying dogs. That is an entirely different and painful chapter.

CHAPTER 9

Hot Days, Sweaty Nights, And Cool Muster

Estate life at Sungai Talam rolled along in an endless succession of numbingly hot days and sweaty, airless nights. The *toc-toc* sounds of the nightjars sent me to sleep in the frightening, noisy silence of the night. The awful clang of my wind up alarm clock shocked me into wakefulness in time for muster. The continuous routine of working on the Estate for most of the day and reading and listening to the radio in my spare time in the evenings, followed by the long uneventful and hot nights became an established pattern of peaceful monotony. Nothing happened outside estate life, because during the first few months after Merdeka Day, I had no transport other than the estate lorry. To use the lorry to take a trip down to the cinema with the old Javanese gardener up on the back as cleaner, also involved a driver. A cinema ticket could be a costly business for me, as both men needed some refreshment while waiting for me to return home. However, to turn up at the Club or to a dinner driven in a Bedford 5-tonner was, for me, slightly embarrassing.

Sungai Talam was my whole life, my entire universe. The days revolved around the events that took place on the estate. The all important early morning roll call started at 5:30 am and was referred to as Muster. A *tindal* or a *mandor* held up a kerosene hurricane lamp in order for Sidek or Mr Thomas to read the names from the check roll. The names were babbled off the conductor's tongue with the speed of a machine gun. Names called out into the early morning darkness like tracers, to ricochet off the temple walls in eerie religious echoes. "Dehivelu, Gnanamuthu, Ganasamy, Jayaraman, Jayakudi..." Tamil male names flowed from Thomas' tongue as hastily as possible, as if a tenth of a second lost was a catastrophe. In the dark chill of the early morning it was like a chant, the list of names was answered in turn, each name acknowledged by some dark, huddling form with a rapid "*Aja.*" When it came to reading out the list of names for the Malay and Tamil female gangs Thomas always seemed to slow down a little. I took it as his way of showing his liking for the female sex. It was an insignificant Thomas concession to the harsh reality of the tough life of an estate labourer. "Aisha, Aminah, Che Mak, Faredah, Zaharah..." the Malay women answered demurely with the Malay word, '*Ada*'. As they answered they turned away, some of them carrying a baby on their hip ready to be placed in the crèche or left in the charge of an elderly relative.

All of us who attended muster, labourers and management, assembled in front of the Hindu temple at the three-way road junction. The contract tappers from Kuantan, who would be transported out to Fields 12 and 13, stayed up on the back of the lorry. The labourers, who shuffled in from the lines like dark uneasy shadows huddled with their arms crossed, hands on their shoulders against the early morning chill; they stood along the fence of the seedling nursery, waiting to hear what task they had been allotted.

From that point in the crossroad, alongside the Hindu temple where we held muster, the unsurfaced road wound its way through the immature rubber trees of RP3 and on out to the main part of the Estate. There were a few small field roads branching off, including the fork leading down the valley to C.J. Windsor's Sungai Tiram Estate. In the opposite direction from the temple the same road led back through the taller trees of RP2 to join the main road between Sungai Lembing and Kuantan. The third, smaller road led up to the office, and on the right-hand side of this road was the estate shop with a light tin roof propped out in front of the shophouse, an uneasy shelter for a table and benches as well as protecting bags of onions, rice, plastic buckets and tins of sweetened condensed milk. Past the shop, the road continued down towards the stream, the Sungai Talam, past a single row of estate labour lines and on to the factory, the packing sheds and the smoke house. The road, which was wide enough for the estate lorry, stopped at the smokehouse where it petered out into a footpath that crossed the narrow river by a single, slippery plank. This path, a more private approach to the estate used by scrap and cup-lump rubber thieves, continued through a field of PB86, the field-budded replant of RP4. From there, the path meandered up the hill and off the estate through a few Malay dwellings and disappeared in a fruit tree orchard, a *dusun*.

The narrow river or stream, flowing in places, in lazy curves and others in shady rapids, came from the hills of the Bukit Goh Forest Reserve and made its way down towards the Kuantan River. It was Sungai Talam. Today, I do not know if it exists or whether it has been boxed in concrete and led underground as a drainage pipe. Then, at least, it ran right through the estate and was the river from which the estate received its name. In the dry season, it was not much more than a gentle trickle over a sand and rock-filled bed. At convenient points close to the factory, the tappers had scooped out the river bed to form pools allowing enough water to accumulate for the washing of working clothes and buckets. In the monsoon it became a totally different fast moving, swirling river. In spate, Sungai Talam could suddenly have a treacherous depth of 10 feet or more, and if you tried to cross and missed your footing you could be carried down the river at frightening speed.

I always thought of muster as a dark and morose affair. All of us were reluctant to leave our beds, one of the reasons being that finally, in the early morning when it was time to get up, the temperature had cooled down enough for our bodies to crave the comfort of a sheet or a light blanket. It is always the best time to sleep, those stolen minutes from the time the alarm rings to the time when we finally manage to make the decision to get out of our beds. In Malaya it meant getting out of bed into the cool darkness of the early morning, the best time of the whole day to sleep. And also a little later, when the dawn exploded with early morning light, it was the best time to enjoy the cool promise of what would be another scorching hot day.

As time went on and muster became such an integral part of my life, the Tamil, Malay and Chinese names that were called out into the early morning blackness soon ceased to be exotic, meaningless sounds. As I came to know the people on the estate I began to put names to their faces. Maurice Cotterill demanded that I should know the name of each and every one of my labour force. Soon, names became faces, the faces and the figures and shapes of my workers, each with his or her special, particular identity and demeanour that it was my business to learn. Some of the women were out-and-out flirts and thereby easy to remember; some of the men were inherently suspicious and hostile, showing it by ignoring me totally or adopting a surly, nasty approach. If I had temporarily forgotten the name of someone I met on a path or on the road or at the office, I would stop and ask them to tell me their name. "*Apa nama*?" I would politely ask.

"*Mariamah, Tuan. Tuan kenal saya, laki saya Muniandy.* My name is Mariamah, sir. Sir, you know me. My husband is called Muniandy."

The names that shot out on the voice of Mr Thomas into the cool morning air of muster eventually attached themselves to the people with whom I worked. Some of them I came to like very much, some I inevitably came to dislike, and I am sure these particular people disliked me. In certain cases, I am of the opinion that the dislike was just a manifestation of the hate of the privilege I represented. Perhaps, simply, the mistrust and envy that exploited labourers have for the bosses. I am also equally sure that certain indications of dislike that sometimes came my way, such as tremors of poorly disguised ill-feeling, or a sideways look, or something I sensed or picked up in an attitude was directed at my age. I was ridiculously young to have so much power, and frighteningly short on experience and knowledge. Sometimes it was quite strange, but I would experience perhaps an instantaneous look of disdain or contempt, not imagined. It might have been an almost imperceptible shrug; a sudden move of the head, a subtle hesitation in obeying an order, I soon discovered that there are so many elusive ways of sending a message. I think these moments, although there were not very many, when a labourer or a tapper, or, indeed, a member of the staff, threw me a sideways glance or allowed me to experience a flash of disdain, a haughty split second of silent disagreement or dislike, these moments were motivated by the hate that any people will show for their oppressors. If I swung round, or glanced up to challenge and to search a face for tell-tale signs of rudeness or plain bolshiness, then, in an instant, any inappropriate look would be gone. I would meet a languid, patient gaze of bland, slightly questioning obsequiousness.

I never had enough evidence to call anyone to task. The extreme cleverness in the way those flashes of contempt were sent in my direction never left me with a remote chance of winning my case. What would I say? That he threw me a malevolent look? I always knew when I had received the look—and the perpetrator always knew there was nothing I could do about it. Except, of course, tuck that knowledge away for future reference, be vigilant and challenge any extra benefits that particular person may accrue. In other words, when dealing with that person, I would assume the mantle of George Wood's artillery of behaviour, and be generally bloody-minded.

Like it or not, in most cases we British were oppressors. We were colonial rulers, in my case, tucked into the commercial enterprise of planting. As British rulers, we had been in control in Malaya for a long time, and therefore were allowed by the passiveness of an oppressed people to develop delusions of benevolent grandeur. So many of us thought we acted in the best interests of the Country. So many of us were able to talk down our own consciences and explain, at least to ourselves, that what we were doing was in the best interests of the people, the country and the estate. In other words we were quick to assume the role of patronising benefactor. My role models were British planters intent on doing a good job and satisfying the Board of Directors in London. Leaving behind them in Malaya a fund of goodwill was not part of their brief or ambition. Having said that, I most sincerely acknowledge that there were many British planters who were genuinely loved by the people under their care.

As the names were called, at those interminable musters, the workers who were present and thereby reporting for work received an entered tick opposite their name and under the appropriate date-column in the pocket check roll. Those who were reported sick, either by turning up themselves or entrusting the task of reporting to a relative, received an 'S' entry in the book. When some of the female names called out were women who were on maternity leave they received an entry of 'M'.

When all the names were entered and the gangs informed of what they would need for the day's tasks, the labourers wandered back to their houses to get ready for work by 6:00 pm. If they were tappers they would collect their knives, sharpening stones, buckets and *kanda* sticks, as well as their sacks or baskets for collection of scrap and cup lump. If they were field workers they collected their *changkuls*, or slashing knives, or tins of Fomac, knapsack sprayers or tins of *lalang* oil. Many of the families who had young children would hand the children to the safekeeping of the crèche (the name given to the day care centre). In the crèche, the youngest infants were suspended in old *sarongs* attached to ropes which were tied to a heavy, spiral metal spring. The up-and -down and swinging movement seemed to have a wonderfully pacifying effect on the children. Older children had to be dressed and ready for school, and also perform some household chores before catching the bus to Atbara Estate and then on to Kuantan, if their parents could afford the school fees, uniforms and books.

After muster, I went back to the bungalow for a cup of coffee before starting my estate work. Maurice never went back to the bungalow. He thought it essential for a planter to proceed immediately from muster out to the various places where the field gangs were to start work. The theory is that one should be there, together with the workers in order to experience what they experience and also to check up on exactly when the gang or group of field workers actually arrived and started work. If they were late, then the *mandor* in charge was supposed to get a severe telling off. I chose to leave that part of running the estate to the conductors. If I noticed something wrong, tardiness in getting started, then I would have a word with Thomas or Sidek and let them sort it out.

That first hour of the morning for the labourers was a difficult time. While I sat in my bungalow and drank coffee, the labourers would be doing all the things necessary in order for them to leave the house for the next six or seven hours. This was the time when small children were woken up and they would walk out of the house to the concrete drain of the five-foot way to urinate or defecate, despite the warning of fines and other terrible threats, as latrines were supplied. Sometimes I would walk back from field visits at breakfast time by way of the lines and see children, and in some cases adults, scuttling away from a drain when they discovered that the *tuan* was walking in their direction. In sympathy with the people who found it more convenient to use the drain outside their house for toilet purposes, it must be said that the borehole latrines with no supply of running water were usually frightful places. It was a constant struggle to get the lines sweeper to make an attempt to clean them up.

After muster, Mr Thomas, Mr Sidek and I strode back up the hill in pitch darkness to the office in order to complete the muster chit by the light of a kerosene lamp. I would cast a remonstrative glance at the queue of labourers who were not going to work. They would be waiting for Sidek to issue them with an aspirin, or follow up on some other treatment. Sidek was always sympathetic and caring and never gave the impression of not believing that a person was sick. Why should he? If they were sick they lost a day's pay.

When the muster chit was completed and I had studied the location of the fields where tapping and other activities were taking place, I walked back up to the bungalow for that early morning cup of coffee—awful instant coffee mixed with overnight hot water from a tatty thermos.

Ah Moi's working day did not start in the house until 7:00 am.

Each evening, after my dinner was served and the dishes cleared away, she used to place a thermos of hot water and a bottle of boiled drinking water on a tray on the glass-topped table in the lounge upstairs. It was the last thing she did, like a small ritual. When she put the tray down, she would walk over to where I was sitting and ask me if there was anything else she could do for me. And then she would say good night.

I usually drank the early morning coffee in silence. It was too early in the day for the English radio broadcast to have started. Sitting upstairs in the open lounge, I could hear the estate coming to life from the faraway sounds of the tappers or labourers calling to each other on their way to work. Through the rolled-up chicks I could watch the delicate but rapid progress of the dawn streak the eastern sky. The early morning coffee and the first cigarette of the day were wonderful minutes of peace and awareness. Birds started to wake up and shrill their territorial messages. The *chik-chaks* in the bungalow noisily advised each other that it was time to pack up for the night and scurried up or down the ceiling in search of a sheltering crevice away from the light. The coolness and the sounds of the night gave way to daytime sounds and the promise of another very hot day. Quite suddenly the sun would be up, like a presence, bursting out in a declaration by the ruler of the day. The earliest rays of the sun painted intense patterns of light and shadow on the jungle trees high up in the Bukit Goh forest reserve of which I could just see a glimpse from the veranda window. It was the time for me, just a little after everyone else, to start my working day.

I usually left the bungalow, walking stick in hand, to go out on my field rounds before Ah Moi was up. When she started work she stripped my bed, collected my dirty washing, swept and polished the floors, dried out my sweaty bed linen in the sun and remade the bed. She performed all these tasks by the time I returned for breakfast somewhere between 9:00 am and 10:00 am. I was taught to stagger my meal times for two reasons. Firstly, for security reasons, if communist terrorists were going to attack or ambush a planter it was sensible for him to never be a creature of habit. Secondly, the labourers themselves would soon come to learn that the *tuan* was in the bungalow at regular times, it would then be tempting for them to take things easy themselves while I ate my breakfast and, later, enjoyed my lunch.

Jahraman's pig

At Sungai Talam Estate one morning, I was sat in the tiny office adding up names in the pocket check roll, getting ready for the book-keeping nightmare of the end of the month wage calculations. The quietness and solitude of the early morning, when everyone was now out in the field, was interrupted when the estate lorry drove up to the office in a cloud of dust and stopped with an unusual jerk. I thought it strange, as Haroun the lorry driver treated his new vehicle with the utmost care. Some very excited tappers rushed up to the door of the office and pleaded with me to go out and help a tapper by the name of Jahraman.

On the back of the lorry was a Tamil who was obviously seriously injured. He was a tapper whose task that morning was in Field 7, close to the jungle. Field 7 was an area of old rubber with some badly overgrown interrow areas full of wild coffee, nephrolepis fern and bracken. The area was scheduled for replanting and undergoing slaughter tapping. We had been stimulating the tapping panels and were using ladders to get at the tappable virgin bark high up on the trees, which were a sorry mess of tapping in every direction

When I climbed up onto the back of the lorry to examine

Jahraman I was shocked to see that the whole of his left leg was covered in blood from his groin all the way down past his knee. He was wearing his working trousers, which were as stiff as a board and covered in weeks and months of coagulated latex so it was difficult to see what was blood and what was material hardened by rubber. I decided that we should lift him off the lorry and we carried him through my office to the examination trestle in the office dispensary. I found some scissors and cut away his trousers, while the excited followers all explained at the same time what had happened. "Babi yang besar sangat, Tuan. Babi itu lari terus kapada Jahraman. *It was the biggest pig you've ever seen, sir. It went straight for Jahraman.* Mat jagga ada lah dekat, dan dia tembak mati babi itu. *The watchman, Mat was close by and he shot and killed the pig."*

When I cut away the material above Jahraman's knee I was horrified to see the whole of his leg opened up, so that the flesh lay pink and bloody on both sides of his femur bone, which I could see, white and large, covered in a bluish but transparent film. I felt sick when I realised the enormity of his wound and frankly I had no idea what to do. As far as I could make out, none of the major arteries or veins was severed. The pig's tusk must have entered at the knee, and, as Jahraman was lifted off the ground by the boar, its tusk had sliced down all the way to the bone through Jahraman's leg ending up at the groin. I guessed it was because the important veins and arteries followed the same direction as the wound that none of them had been cut or severed. I had never seen a wound like it. Jahraman was in deep shock and, even though none of his arteries were damaged, some of the smaller veins and capillaries were pumping or oozing blood. His lips were frighteningly pale; I could tell from the pallor of his dark skin that he had lost quite a lot of blood and I guessed that his blood pressure was probably dangerously low.

Sungai Talam Estate, 1958. Michael Thorp (author) with the wild boar that attacked Jahraman.

Even to me, with tremendously limited medical knowledge it was obvious that Jahraman was hovering on the edge of unconsciousness. His head was lolling aimlessly from side to side, and his eyes were staring without really seeing. I tried to reassure him as best I could. I realised that it was vitally important that he should be taken to hospital as soon as possible. Trying to sound resourceful and confident I barked out an instruction to the onlookers to run down and fetch 20 or 30 empty gunny sacks from the packing shed to make a more comfortable platform for him on the back of the lorry. I ran as fast as I could to the bungalow to fetch some of my own clean towels. To Ah Moi's surprise I stormed into the bungalow and up the stairs to grab a couple of large white bath towels. Breathless, but back at the office, I instructed Sidek, who had heard the news and managed to get back from the field, to gently lift Jahraman's injured leg. I tucked the end of the towel under his leg and wound the rest of the towel as tight as I could like a bulky bandage carefully bringing the two grotesque flaps of flesh back together. We carried him back out to the lorry and placed him on a mattress of gunny-sacks that would at least cushion some of the bumps on the road to Kuantan.

He was given half a cup of sweetened tea that someone had fetched for him from the shop. Sidek went with him in the lorry and I instructed two men to sit up on the back to support the casualty. Haroun, the Malay lorry driver swung himself up into the cab and drove off to the Kuantan District Hospital some ten miles away.

Later that afternoon, when the lorry had finished latex collection Vadiveloo, the reserve driver and some companions drove out to Field 7 and picked up the pig. They took it back to the office. Haroun, of course, being Malay could not touch it. I have a photo of myself squatting by the side of the wild boar, sizing him up. That evening I received a gift of a saucepan of chilli-hot curried wild boar, which I had for dinner. The contents of the saucepan were shared with Ah Moi and the Javanese gardener. Ah Moi later told me that as a Muslim, the gardener had made her swear silence before he would eat it. Hunger is difficult to live with. Many of the Tamils and Chinese living at Sungai Talam must have eaten wild boar that evening. Jahraman recovered but had an enormous scar on his leg. And if he is still alive, he will be able to show that scar, and tell his story to his grand children.

I never got my towels back.

CHAPTER 10

Motorcycle And Liberation

After several months of living and working on Sungai Talam Estate I saved enough money to buy a motorcycle. I bought it from a Chinese workshop on Bukit Ubi Road. The owner was called Ah Heng, and I was warned that he was a bit sharp. It was a Triumph 200 c.c. Tiger cub with a silver tank and it went like a rocket.

I am reluctant to admit, but at the same time still a little proud, to say that I managed the trip from my bungalow to the Ganesh temple on Bukit Ubi Road in seven and a half minutes. This distance of seven miles was quite tricky for a motorcycle rider. The first section belonged to the estate. I had to follow the unmade dirt road and negotiate the plank bridge over the Sungai Talam at something like reasonable speed, as some of the corners were totally blind because of overhanging branches and creepers, and it was impossible to tell if another vehicle was approaching. At the bridge itself, both approaches were frighteningly steep down one side and up the other. The bridge was constructed by two main logs laid staight across the river and a series of slats running parallel to the river. On top there were three planks placed side by side wide enough to facilitate the wheels of a lorry. The driver of a Landrover, even though it had a wide wheelbase, often had difficulty in keeping both sets of wheels on the planks. I always chose the left side planks when riding away from the estate and had both wheels off the ground when I reached the other side of the bridge. Immediately after the bridge, there was a sharp right-hand bend up a steep slope to a point where the estate road joined the Sungai Lembing to Kuantan Road. This was the main road into Kuantan. It had a laterite surface for most of its distance until it reached the Ganesh temple, where the tarmac surface of the town limit started, and I had to slow down.

I still ride a motorcycle today for pure pleasure and convenience. When I think back to those mad dashes into town, I have no idea why I should have wanted to do it, except that wild blood bubbles like champagne in the veins of most young men. No crash helmet, no protective clothing—completely idiotic young man's behaviour.

I remember the enormous bugs, attracted to my headlight when riding back to the Estate at night. They would sometimes bang into my forehead and my face with a sharp, painful crack and I would be suddenly aware of that peculiarly pungent, leafy smell of squashed flying beetles in my nostrils.

The motorcycle opened up a different world. After months of very quiet living on the Estate, where I stayed home almost every evening, I was suddenly able to accept invitations, and even more important get to Telok Cempedak for a swim in the ocean. The Tiger Cub meant that at last I could attend functions in the Kuantan Club, and be able to accept invitations to play in cricket matches. Quite suddenly, my life opened up into a whole different world. The motorcycle was like a magic carpet, noisily roaring me off into a whirl of bachelor living that was fun and somewhat expensive. Even so, I am sure that having my own transport, at last, saved me from becoming a recluse or resigning from my job at the age of twenty-one.

Because of my newly found freedom, brought to me by my motorbike, I started to make friends with other young European men in the Kuantan district. Men like me, who were bachelors. These unmarried men carried that quaint bachelor label with an aura of nonchalant irresponsibility. In a pathetic way we thought it amusing to deceive ourselves into thinking that we represented a potential challenge to any women, married or unmarried between the ages of seventeen and forty. The term, bachelor also included the European married men who were separated for some reason from their wives. This lent them the predatory title of 'bachelor' and, while the wife was away, they often attracted the attention of the married women in the Club. A lifted, speculative eyebrow, a quick glance, unusually long pressure of a hand resting on an arm. If the truth be known, I suppose some European bachelors were a genuine threat to the well-being and harmonious marriages of many European couples, particularly those where the husband was frequently out-station.

Owning a motorcycle meant that for the first time I was able to meet young Planters from neighbouring estates. I was able to mix freely with young PWD engineers and people from the commercial branches of trading and banking. Commercial people, they were decidedly different from us planters, as they had no idea of the Malay language, and were isolated from what we considered to be real contact with the country. As planters, we tended to look down on them slightly, for their transient existence, which in our minds, demonstrated a lack of commitment to the Country.

For the first time I was able to discuss and compare working and living conditions with other European men. Most of the people I met at that time were supplied with some form of transport. If they were planters, they had a company Land Rover; if they were government employees or commercial people, they were given an interest-free loan and were able to purchase a car. It seemed that only Kuala Reman Rubber Estates and the Borneo Company, who, at that time were our agents, were mean and short-sighted enough to withhold transportation from their young European assistants. Today, of course, I would most certainly blame the manager. I am absolutely sure that if Maurice had thought far enough, indeed, thought anything about his young European staff, he would have insisted that they be given transport. It could have been limited when it came to private use to something like thirty or forty gallons of petrol a month, but at least we would have had transport. I think this awful oversight demonstrated a shocking lack of consideration and responsibility. I am sure that there is not one single young assistant manager in the plantation industry in Malaysia today who would accept being posted to an isolated and lonely estate without adequate transport. For the management of estates to keep young European employees tucked away in isolation, miles from any contact with other people with whom they had, at least, their cultural heritage in common, demonstrated an almost criminal negligent failing to take proper, reasonable and necessary care of their staff.

Transport, in the form of my motorcycle also meant that I would be in a position, together with other young men, to explore the impossibly dull night life that Kuantan offered in 1957–1958. At that time it was almost unheard of for European men (again, I refer mainly to the British) to go out with Asian, that is to say, local girls.

There was much more stigma attached from the Asian side than from the European side. The British certainly tolerated that their men had affairs with Asian women, but these men were expected to follow an unwritten code of behaviour; that is to be discreet—not flaunt the women and the relationship, for example by taking them to the Club. Many, if not the majority of British planters at one time or other had a local girl as a 'keep', but they left them in the bungalow and never ever referred to them in polite company. This 'discretion' also afforded some measure of protection for the woman the planter lived with, so that she did not become the object of gossip and chatter in the Club. It meant that she herself could retain some dignity. Many of these women were vitally important in the lives of their men. Some planters actually married their 'keep' and some were eventually nominated in the wills and testaments of the men they lived with as a common law wife. In almost all cases during social visits by other Europeans to the bungalow of a planter who had a local girlfriend, particularly if '*mems*' were among the visitors, the local girl stayed in the background. However, if you became a frequent guest and a good friend of the *tuan*, then, perhaps, the 'keep' would appear and join in the conversation. It would be an incredibly interesting task to try to document the lives that some of these women had, and the influence they had on their men. And, as I know happened in so many cases, to document the tragically sad fates that most of these women suffered when their *tuans* left the country and abandoned them.

In the 1950s and 1960s, Asian parents of young women were horrified if they heard or witnessed that their daughters were seen talking to, or even thinking about talking to, young European men. Asians, with good reason, were of the unshakable belief that young unmarried European men, if pursuing a young Asian girl were only after one thing; to seduce and thereby ruin the girl and her reputation; and when the European tired of her, the girl would be abandoned and left to run back to her family with no chance of making a decent marriage. Unfortunately, events often proved that young European men were interested in a good time, but perhaps not so keen in making an honest woman of an Asian girlfriend. Parents, more often than not, were much wiser than their daughters.

Naturally, European bachelors thirsted for the comfort

and warmth of female companionship, and they were often looking for sexual encounters. This need, this longing for female companionship and warmth, and feminine contact was exacerbated by the extreme loneliness and inherent danger of living as a planter on an isolated estate. However, for Asians, particularly in the 1950s, virginity was an essential requirement in order for a girl to make a good marriage. This prerequisite applied to all three main ethnic groups; the Malays, the Chinese and the Indians. In addition, a Malay girl who was seen to go out with a young man, alone with him in a car, or on the beach, or any situation with him in what the Muslim clergy sensibly refers to as close proximity or *khalwat*, would incur enormous problems for the girl and her parents.

The policing of *khalwat* is still vigorously pursued in Malaysia today, in, however, I suspect, slightly more lenient terms. For a Malay girl to go out with a non-Muslim at that time would mean big trouble for her and severe problems for him. Problems which could be resolved by his conversion to Islam and a swift and quiet marriage, if the couple are serious enough and the relationship has reached the stage that warrants such measures.

Call it what you like, but in the 1950s the young British men, sent out to a British colony to do a job, were a long way from home. They were lonely and, as far as planters were concerned, there was still an edge of danger from the lingering threat of communist terrorists. Loneliness, danger, languid and tortuously hot nights exacerbates the forces that drive men in their hungry needs. The need to put one's arms around a woman, in a country that has an abundance of the world's most beautiful and feminine women, was, on occasions irresistible. At that time it could frequently be a recipe for disaster. Asian women have a very special appeal to European men. Unlike their Western counterparts, they have retained that special allure which is femininity. They are petite, with beautiful tiny figures, attractive eyes and beautiful hair, which they know instinctively how to use in a femininely alluring way.

Today, many Asian girls are extremely well-educated in their own right, and they continue, without sacrificing their feminine dignity, to continue to be alluringly feminine and attractive. Femininity, if I were asked to enlarge or define exactly what I mean by the word, is when a woman appeals to a man in all the most sensuous and intellectual ways. A feminine woman instinctively knows when her signals are being well received. Often, the feminine woman appears to be unaware of the attention, and this in itself is enough to captivate a man and, her apparent indifference somehow invests her with an added attraction. It is the way a woman consciously and unconsciously demonstrates her femaleness. It would seem that Western women have sacrificed something of their femininity. It is confused with intelligence. Educated Western women think they lose something of value if they exercise their femininity. However, many of their Asian sisters still retain something special, in a world where competition between the sexes seems to be obliterating the differences.

Having a supply of young, healthy and good-looking British bachelors in the district also led to an enormous amount of flirting within the European community. At Club nights, bachelors danced with mature married women and whispered sweet nothings that were desperate outpourings of the yearnings of libidinous young men. The women blushed to hear such things and pushed themselves in closer to hear even more. I remember dancing with a beautiful Australian woman who must have been at least fifteen years older than me, telling her that she was the most beautiful woman in the room, and that I was madly in love with her. Even she, who should have known better, pretended to swoon in my arms at the same time imploring me to let her have more intimate details. It was a game. Just as flirting has

British High Commisioner Sir Geoffrey Tory's visit to The Kuantan Club, 1958.
Top, from left to right: Michael Thorp (author), Lady Tory, Rugiah Emery from Singapore, Helen Wharton, Sir Geoffrey Tory, Johnnie Liew (who went on to become Datuk Liew), and an unidentified person from Kuala Lumpur.
Bottom, from left to right: Maurice Cotterill M.B.E., Sir Geoffrey Tory, and Datuk Abdullah, Mentri Besar, Pahang.

always been a game. But, sometimes, couples stepped over the mark and they ended up on the beach or in the back seat of an uncomfortable car parked on some lonely estate road.

Young, married British husbands were often quite desperate in their efforts at keeping predatory bachelors away from their women. Some of these unfortunate husbands were given nicknames by the bachelors. There was one in Kuantan, who received the nickname, the 'Mad Mullah'. He was an engineer in the Drainage Department married to a ravishingly beautiful girl from Singapore. On Club social evenings, if there was music, this girl was a delight to dance with, as, not only did she have the figure and face of a beauty queen but she would press her exquisite body close into you in such a way that a reaction was inevitable. When she felt that reaction, she would lean back, pushing her body even closer, and say, "You are a naughty boy." She would look into your eyes and smile and then say, "But I shall take it as a compliment." After dancing with this beautiful and dangerous woman, the bachelors would group at the bar and, with a knowing lift of an eyebrow, ask each other if they had managed to give her a 'compliment'. Her unhappy husband, earning his nickname, would be sitting in a chair glowering at events until he could stand it no longer. Watching his wife pushing her body close to yet another man would eventually make him march furiously onto the dance floor, grasp his wife by her wrist and storm out of the Club. While this disgraceful display of matrimonial squabbling was taking place, the bachelors retreated to the farthest end of the bar in order to watch events, and just in case the 'Mad Mullah' decided to come back looking for trouble after locking his wife in their car. Like young seals on a cliff when facing an angry bull, the young men felt there was safety in numbers.

I was, in many ways, too young to join wholeheartedly in

the desperate, bachelor pursuit of the available and unavailable women in Kuantan. Besides, at that time in the desperate months of loneliness on the Estate, when my emotional life must have been in a state of imbalance, I wrote an impassioned letter and proposed marriage to the woman I left behind in England. This act of commitment required me to eschew other female involvements; at least, according to the Boy Scout code, I felt it prudent and correct to follow and remember. I must have been insufferable.

It would not be historically correct if I were to avoid mentioning the names of some of the people who were in the Kuantan district. From Jabor Valley Estate I made a friend who has been a friend all my life, Peter Stone. Peter served in Malaya with the British Army before he started life as a planter. There was also another young Englishman stationed on Jabor Valley, Simon Pearson. He was a keen photographer. After serving his first contract on Jabor he left Malaya for Australia. To my knowledge, he left at least one broken heart behind. I have never heard from him since. Bill Dishington was the Scottish Manager of The Mercantile Bank, which is now the HSBC Bank. Today, it is a busy air-conditioned bank offering services that were unheard of in 1958. The dentist, Johnnie Liew and Bill Dishington were good friends, and at that time, Johnnie was a bachelor. Before opening his dental practice in Kuantan and going on to become a much respected citizen and a *datuk*, he had been in government service as a dentist in the Kemaman district. Occasionally, all of us bachelors would meet up with some of the young men in government service and the young men from the Police Field Force Unit at Alor Akar, where there was an excellent small club and the beer was cheap. This mixing of the races was wonderful. We were Europeans and Asians, all reasonably educated, and we

Occasion with the Kuantan Police Field Force at the East Pahang Police Officers'
Mess, Kuantan, 1958. From left to right: Police Lieutenant Stevenson; Michael Thorp
(author), BIll Dishington, Manager, Mercantile Bank; Brother Aloysius, Teacher, St.
Thomas School; Simon Pearson, Planter, Jabor Valley Estate.

were experiencing our first really honest feelings of equality, the
beginnings of true friendship and appreciation. For some hours
the Europeans managed to drop their feelings of superiority
and opened up to learn, and the Asians dropped their feelings
of hostility and reluctance to open up to the process of mutual
understanding.

I suppose it would be correct to say, and we all need some
excuse, that it was not until I joined in the more racy side of
bachelor life in Kuantan that I started drinking beer. We drank
Tiger or Anchor beer in the Moonlight Hotel, which also served

excellent *mee goreng* late at night; we visited the Planet Hotel, we visited Aziz Café in Bukit Ubi Road for excellent *halal* curries, we ate Chinese-Thai *pow* and *dim sum* at the eating stalls close by the side of the Cathay Cinema on Bukit Ubi Road, and we were frequent visitors in the Chinese eating stalls in the market. These stalls were situated in what was until recently a combination of parking for vehicles and a small fruit market in the centre of town, on the south side of Jalan Mahkota, opposite the *padang* and the mosque. In their place today is an enormous building on the site, testimony to the vigorous property development business that is taking place in Kuantan.

Rats were a problem in the market stalls. Large and well-fed, they used to scuttle along the drains where there was a plentiful supply of washed down rice and uneaten bones. They were so well-fed and urban that they were slow to move, and only reluctantly dived for cover if you were almost on top of them. But the food was excellent. It was prepared on charcoal fires as this was long before the convenience of gas for the woks, and electricity for the rice cookers. And you could get an excellent meal as late as midnight. We were well known by the Chinese stall proprietors, which in effect meant being to some extent recognised and tolerated.

Sitting at those stalls late at night, it was not difficult to understand that we Europeans were not subjects of affection for the Chinese stall keepers. The service comprised solely of an obviously reluctant *towkay* scuffling up to our table in worn-out rubber slippers, and demanding, with a jerk of his head, what we wanted to eat. These *towkays* were usually hostile and surly, and their wives, who were in the stalls to help, simply turned away from us. But, a customer is a customer. In addition, the Chinese men who were our fellow customers (women were never seated at the stalls as far as I can remember), were not too fond of seeing us, in what was essentially a Chinese preserve. The amount of spitting would somehow increase. We knew we were talked about, and judging from the sullen and sneering looks on faces, it was not difficult to work out that the general Chinese attitude towards us was not complimentary.

I remember one particular evening, when we did see a young Chinese woman sitting in the eating stalls. She was quite beautiful, with an unusual coppery glint to her hair. I found it difficult to stop myself taking glances in her direction. From someone in our group, we were informed that she was known as, 'the fisherman's whore'. She had, apparently, been brought over to Kuantan from Kuala Lumpur and had been earning a lot of money in fairly high-class circles, including some European clients. But, seemingly, she had drifted into a drug and liquour problem, perhaps to make her life more bearable, and it soon came to be known that she was living life very fast, and was not quite as particular in terms of health as she had been.

It was said that the fishermen paid her well, and that they probably had the best access to *chandu* in the whole district. Nothing is easier than to haul up a load of something other than crabs in your nets if you agree the location of the marker buoy.

I watched her as she sat on a chair at one of the tables, laughing. Her foot was tucked up under her thigh, the tight material of her *sam foo* showing every man for miles that she had a gorgeous figure. I was totally fascinated, but at the same time horrified. In my 30th Reigate Boy Scout Troop and Reigate Grammar School code of ethics, honour, and decent behaviour, I knew that to go with a 'dirty' woman was the road to hell. At the same time, I terrified myself by wondering what it would be like to pay $20 and explore her body.

Monsoon

The rainfall gauge at Sungai Talam was situated at an open spot next to the multiplication nursery away from interfering trees and buildings. We measured and entered records of rainfall every morning at 7:00 am. In December 1957, we measured 57 inches of rain in 31 days. During one 24-hour period, we received 12.57 inches of rain. I remember the figures; 57 inches was so easy to link to the year, 1957. The figures have stuck in my head, locked in the recesses of my brain that have also logged and catalogued the memory of that rain-soaked and dismal month.

During the monsoon of 1957, many houses at Pasir Kemudi, a village situated on the west bank of the Kuantan river halfway between Kuantan and Sungai Lembing, were washed away and people were temporarily given shelter in the village school and other buildings nearby. The Charu River, on the road to Sungai Lembing at Kolek, was running so high that all road traffic to the mining community was cut off for days on end. In countless places, the flow of water washed away entire sections of road. The ferry across the Kuantan River, which was the main road connection to Kuala Lumpur, was also halted because the enormous flow of the river, and the debris of torn-out tree trunks, coconut fronds and large sections of swamp grass carried along by the floodwaters made it unsafe to operate. The ferry was winched across the river on a wire system, and it was both impossible and too dangerous to attempt the crossing. All the way up the East Coast there were terrible floods. All the ferries up to Kelantan were unable to operate because of the fast-flowing and dangerously flooding rivers. Many communities were entirely cut off from the rest of the world.

During the whole of that December we could only attempt tapping on 12 days, and eight of those days were washed out. When latex from a hundred thousand trees drips insistently into the clay cups, and the tappers are getting ready to collect it, the worst thing that can happen is a 'wash-out'; that is when the clouds open, and the monsoon rain pours down with such force and intensity that the tapping panels are soaked in minutes. The latex, which has filled the cups is quickly diluted by the rain running down the trunks of soaked trees. The wet ferocity of an incessant monsoon downpour washes latex away completely.

During the monsoon season, everything is damp. Bed linen is damp even though you keep the louvered shutters to the bedroom firmly closed. Your towels are never dry, and mould forms on shoes in the cupboards. The leather attaché case I carried with me to go and collect money twice a month from the bank would be covered in a whitish mycelium powder, and my washing hardly got dry. The noise of the rain was incessant and depressing. We had no such thing as air-conditioning. When the chill and the damp became really bad we would fire up a chattie; a small, charcoal-burning stove made of clay, and put it on the floor of the lounge on an underlay of bricks. The smoky heat somehow took the edge off the damp air and countered the chill of sitting in a sunless bungalow, with all the chicks down, against the beating rain. Endlessly gloomy days when listening to the radio was an impossibility, and one seemed to spend hours captive to the booming monotonous music of rain beating down on the roof and torrents of water pouring from overloaded gutters and drains.

The Sungai Talam was, for days, a raging, turbid, surging, frightening river. For days on end, we could not drive a vehicle off the Estate, as the road-bridge was several feet under water. We cleared all the rubber from the smokehouse and checked every last ounce of stock in bales and loose sheets in the packing shed. It was the only work we could undertake; everything else came to a standstill. In those days, the daily paid workers received little or no compensation for lost wages due to the weather. There was nothing for the workers to do except sit under eaves of the lines and watch the rain wrap the world in a blanket of water. We baled every sheet of rubber we could find and thoroughly cleaned the factory, the smokehouse and the packing shed.

With so many rainy days, there was little or no tapping work, and almost no fieldwork going on. When we decided to have a thorough check and weigh all the rubber we had in stock, I spent an unusual amount of time in the packing shed. A favourite place to stand was by the ramp that led up to the smokehouse. Aminah, one of our rubber sorters, worked at the same spot at a bench facing the open shutters. She bent down and picked up sheet after sheet of rubber, placing it on an opaque glass plate in order to find and clip out, with large shears, bits of bark, sand, and other impurities.

Aminah's family was from Java, and she dressed more like a Javanese girl than a Malay girl. Her sarong was always colourful and clean, even in the packing shed, and it hugged her beautifully slender shape. The bodice or blouse reached just to the hip and would be made of a different colour to her sarong, the front always low-cut and incredibly enticing. Aminah had nothing against teaching me Malay words and flirting with me at the same time. I received glances from Aminah that made me uncomfortable in a pleasant way. But Aminah was married, and I had to content myself with sneaking glances down her cleavage. She knew that I enjoyed looking at her and she certainly did not mind. In fact, she would linger in front of me when bending down to pick up another sheet of rubber. Then, at the age of twenty, I relished moments with Aminah and those wonderfully informative and pleasant Malay lessons she gave me, correcting my pronunciation with pursed lips and a flashing smile. If Thomas or Sidek showed up in the packing shed, I would immediately straighten up and be the tuan, and Aminah would assume a more professional approach to the business of sorting ribbed smoked sheets.

CHAPTER 11

Telok Cempedak

In those days, in 1957, when I first saw the beach at Telok Cempedak, it took my breath away. I really found it difficult to breathe; it was so beautiful. It was like kissing; I held my breath. I immediately fell in love with the place, with an aching sensation of wanting to reach out and fold the trees, the sand, the water and the wind into my very soul. My first view was a revelation, a major happening in my life. The beauty of the place has stamped itself into my consciousness. Today, if I close my eyes, I can picture the gentle curve of the bay, the granite rocks at each end, the frothy line of waves and the deeper blue-green water. I can hear it, smell it, and it fills me with a longing and a happiness that is unbearable.

At that time, Telok Cempedak was devoid of any type of building. The Kuantan Merlin Hotel, which no longer exists, was undreamed of; the small Chinese-owned Kuantan Hotel, and the internationally famous Hyatt were years away from the drawing board. The shophouses on the left-hand side, as you drive over the crest of the hill and approach the beach, and the houses at the main road turn-off, including the Istana, which was built for the present Sultan when he was the Tengku Mahkota, were non-existent. The *taman*, the golf course and the expensive flats at Kuantan Tembiling did not exist either. The whole area was wild country and the swampy land between Jalan Telok Sisek and Jalan Beserah was undrained jungle.

C.J. Windsor and his wife, Edna, told me that they were walking on the beach early one morning, before the Japanese occupation, when, for several minutes, they watched a female honey bear with two cubs investigating the beach for washed-up fish. There are tiger stories relating to the beach but these are now forgotten. People like Datuk Mohamad, a wonderful and kind gentleman, who was the first Menteri Besar after Independence, had a fund of tiger stories. He was an enthusiastic hunter of birds for the pot. He told me that he had seen leopard pugmarks close to the beach. These wonderful stories are disappearing along with the people who are able to recount them.

"How do you relate killing birds with a shot gun to the Muslim requirement to slaughter?" I once impertinently asked him.

He looked at me kindly, obviously understanding that youth has much to learn. "Well, Michael, when we hunt, we hunt for food. Not for trophy. I abhor trophy killing." he said. "And, when I pull the trigger, I pull the trigger in the name of Allah. He who supplies us with all the wonder and bounty of this world." His calm reply taught me a lesson. It gave me an insight into what tolerance really is, and what respect for other life really means. I remember him today, as I write. However briefly he touched my life I am grateful for his brush marks.

Bernard Preedie was an Englishman who had spent his adult life as a teacher in some of the schools in Pahang. He was the first person to be allowed to put up a building on the beach at Telok Cempedak. It was a sort of house combined with headquarters for the Sea Scouts. In recognition of his many years of work in Pahang as a teacher, Preedie was given permission by Sultan Abu Bakar to build a house and live in retirement on the beach. The Sultan permitted Preedie's request in acknowledgement of Preedie's efforts, and for his work with the Boy Scouts. Preedie's house was the very first building to be erected on the beach and I am reasonably sure that this took place in 1962.

There were rumours about Preedie, just as there are rumours about any unmarried man who has spent a lifetime in teaching at schools where boys are the pupils. Boarding schools, frightening places, where little boys are sent to achieve an all-round education. Where little boys, and for that matter little girls, seek companionship and warmth and relief from their homesickness. Where little children are prey to the whims of adult teachers who are specifically employed in order to look after young impressionable children who often feel that they have been rejected and sent away. So many children of the Europeans working in Malaya and other British colonies were sent off to boarding schools. Many of these children grew up to become adults who harbour unhappy memories.

I remember Preedie's house. It looked like a Malay village house, built of dark-coloured timber and was relatively simple in design. I am sure that it was situated almost exactly where the small Kuantan Hotel used to be just opposite the entrance to today's Hyatt Regency.

I also remember once eating a meal with Bernard Preedie in his house on the beach. I was so impressed by the practicality of the round Chinese dining table with the superbly efficient 'lazy Susan' in the middle. Chinese dining tables are almost always circular. The Chinese are very practical. You can sit more people in less space at a circular table. The Chinese serve their different foods in dishes placed close to the centre of the table. People sitting at the table have their own small bowl, a spoon and chopsticks. They help themselves to rice and reach for the contents of the dishes of fish, meat and vegetables with their chopsticks. Some tables are equipped with a large circular plate, mounted on heavy-duty ball bearings in the middle of the table. The whole disc can be rotated in order for the diners to pull in front of them the dish they choose and then they are able in turn to select with their chopsticks from all the dishes on the table. Preedie, if he wanted something to be passed to him, sauce or chillies for example, would say, "Put it on the train." The item would then be placed on the circular disk in the middle of the table and the disk, the lazy Susan, given a gentle push.

Preedie told me that he had seen a black leopard on the beach at Telok Cempedak, and, at night, he had heard a noise best described as the sawing sound of a tiger. At that time, Telok Cempedak beach was wild and fiercely beautiful, and jungle stretched to the north and the south for many uninterrupted miles.

To get to the beach, it was best to use a Land Rover, as the track was only used by a few net-casting fishermen, who fished the tidal flats in the shallower bay to the north. The Malays also fished the waters of the bay, from small sail-assisted boats that, today, have totally disappeared.

The Europeans who did drive down to the beach usually turned off to the right and headed south. That turn-off was at the point where the drive-in McDonalds is so commercially situated today. If you continued parallel to the beach, past where the Hyatt is now situated, you would arrive at a clump of delightful casuarina trees. This was an unofficial and usual parking space for the European people who used the beach.

I am unable to recall any incident of theft or interference with the cars or personal belongings, except occasionally you might see a monkey with his backside sticking out of any open car windows. Today, I am desperately sad to see that there are relatively few casuarinas on the beach, and at our parking spot there is now a dismal ghost-project of a hotel, occupied by monkeys who have the freedom to come and go as they please.

It looms up from the jungle behind the beach, forcing its way out like a lost city from the beautiful forest trees behind. It is a sad monument to commercial greed. Something should be done in the interests of international tourism. Perhaps it would be best to tear the whole building down and assist the area in reverting to its natural state. Failing this, the building could be used for an amended project to develop holiday flats or condominiums. I think well-off tourists from western countries would pay good sums of money for the privilege of living on that beautiful beach during the European winters.

It is a tragedy to think that a well-developed hotel like the Kuantan Merlin was pulled down in favour of a monstrosity. The Merlin at least had individual chalets, where one could stay and watch the South China Sea continuously pounding its waves on the beach. The hotel section, which was behind the chalets, was of good enough standard to challenge the present-day commercial monopoly of the Hyatt. The dining room was pleasant and afforded a view of the beach. This has all been pulled down to make way for an over-dimensioned and out-of-place concrete monument to badly researched tourist and local demand. It is a project that has run out of money, blamed, of course, on the slump in world trade and speculation in currency, which prompted the then Malaysian Prime Minister, Dr Mahathir, to introduce some tough monetary reforms. I understand that there are plans do something with it, and I am tempted to suggest that anything would be better than just leaving it to rot and moulder, looking like a film set from a Disney production of Jungle Book.

I love Telok Cempedak, and have watched it change from being a pristine, untouched natural wonder to a place that will soon compare to a McDonalds-invaded Blackpool. The best beach on the East Coast is on the edge of becoming over-exploited and vulgar. I beg the Malaysian authorities to be prudent in the development and use of their coastal beauty spots. Of course, this wonderful beach should be a place of recreation and enjoyment for the local population. To bring in more and more foreign tourists and build even larger hotels will overload the facilities, and very soon the place will get a bad name. Even the beach itself is under threat, and millions of *ringgits* have been spent on efforts at rehabilitation.

The joy of Telok Cempedak is, quite simply, the timeless appeal of a special bay, where the wonder of the tropical rainforest and sand meet the incredible miracle of the ocean. The eternal and timeless miracle of Telok Cempedak is for us to be able to enjoy the peace that immeasurable beauty brings, and to have the opportunity to allow natural forces of wind, sky and ocean, and the perfume of the forest to surround us and remind us of the sheer bounty of this world.

River in spate

In 1960, I was Assistant-in-charge of Nada Estate, a 2000-acre division of Kuala Reman Rubber Estates. Nada is halfway between Panching and Sungai Lembing, and at that time, it was a fairly lonely and desolate posting. The Charu River runs through the estate flowing north on its way to join the Kuantan River. In 1960, the Charu River water was clear and good to swim in, and I often took an evening dip or played with Barney and my other dog, a dog I inherited from a couple called Shaw, the husband an employee of PCCL. They handed the dog, a half-blind boxer called Major, over to me, because none of us fancied the idea of having the dog destroyed when they returned to England.

The road bridge over the Charu River was a low-level bridge situated on the road to Sungai Lembing. The advantage of a low-level bridge is that when a river floods it brings down with the floodwater enormous loads of fallen trees, logs and other debris. All this flotsam, if it were to pack up against the bridge, would mean that the enormous pressure of water would eventually push the bridge until it breached or was carried away by the swollen river. With a low-level bridge, all this debris can pass safely over the top.

In December 1960, the Charu flooded. My bungalow and all the Estate buildings were on the Sungai Lembing side of the river, so the floods meant that we were all cut off from Kuantan until the water subsided. Most of our buildings, except the Ampang lines were safe from floods. My own bungalow was a large two-storey building on top of a hill. It was the same building occupied by George Wood when the baby elephant in the garage incident occurred.

When the river flooded, I would drive down in my Land Rover periodically to record whether the floodwaters were rising or subsiding. This information I relayed to the mine and to George Wood who was then my Manager and based at Panching. One morning, at the beginning of the flood period I arrived at the bridge to see a queue of lorries and cars. The drivers were standing looking at the floodwater flowing over the bridge and wondering whether or not to try to cross or turn back.

Eventually, the Chinese driver of a lorry with good clearance and a load of timber weighing it down decided to try. The bridge was covered by almost two feet of fast flowing water. He revved his engine and nosed into the floodwaters and passed over safely, but I am sure I saw the back end of the lorry drift a little when the back wheels and the submerged parts of the vehicle encountered the strongest part of the current.

In the queue of vehicles waiting to cross the river was an Indian man. I think he was a schoolteacher and had been visiting someone in Sungai Lembing. He had with him his wife and two fairly young children. He also decided to attempt to cross. When he reached me on the approach to the water I signalled him to stop.

"Don't do it!" I shouted, with my voice thin and reedy in the noise from the river. "You cannot cross, not in your car." His car was a small black Austin Ten, relatively new. He chose to completely ignore the warning, and to my horror I watched him drive the car out across the bridge its front wheels plunging into the water. He was past the middle of the bridge, when quite suddenly, the car was just lifted off the bridge and floated downstream at a surprisingly fast speed. As the car was swept off the edge of the bridge it was swung round in the full force of the current to face downstream and I could see the look of horror on his wife's face. The vehicle, caught in snags, trapped on the bottom of the river. It sank so that the water was halfway up the doors, nose tipped forward in the river, got caught up again on something but was lifted clear, and carried on down the river, tilting and half-submerged in the furious waters.

I had no choice. I plunged into the river and started swimming as fast as I could after the car. Fortunately, the car grounded on a flat area of land but it was almost completely under water and filling up through the open windows. I grabbed one child at a time, part-swam, part-waded to the bank and pushed the children up. I went back for the woman, who was by now out of the car and hanging desperately on to the open door. I grabbed her and took her to her children. By then I was exhausted and I turned to look at the car just in time to see it completely disappear in the water. The driver, the Indian teacher, was in the river and he managed to drag himself out about 50 yards downstream.

"You are mad," I shouted at him angrily. "You risked drowning your wife and children even though you must have known it was too dangerous to try." He turned away from me, and together with his wife and children, he started to walk towards the safety of the road. "Silly bastard," I shouted after him. He turned and looked back at me with anger in his glance.

I was now on the wrong side of the river, and did not relish the struggle to get back across the river to my Land Rover. The teacher never wrote and thanked me, of course not. Even though I may have saved the life of his children, I belittled him by insulting him, and many times, thinking about that incident, I am sorry. My anger got the better of me, but it was prompted by fear. Fear for his children and fear for him and his wife, and of course I was afraid for myself. If he ever reads this then I would like to apologise for my arrogant behaviour.

CHAPTER 12

Cricket On The Padang Besar And The Kuantan Recreation Club

In 1958 Harry Wharton, an Australian entomologist, was working for the Government on elephantiasis research and the study of the mosquito-born disease, filariasis. Barry Laing, a British doctor was working on the same project, which was designed to understand the vectors and nature of the disease and thereby learn more in order to bring about its eradication.

Harry was a tall, good-looking man with a thin moustache, tanned from the sun, athletic and an excellent cricketer. On the cricket field he was a tiger; each ball was a new opportunity and if you were fielding on his side you had to stay awake. Barry was a quieter, more intellectual and reserved Englishman, always well turned out. Where Harry was brown from his outdoor life, Barry was pale; he stayed out of the sun. However, he offered lots of support. He would load up his car with bats, and pads, and ice for the drinks, and he would see to it that the scoreboard was in place, but he did not play.

The arch enemy—no, that is too severe—the arch-rival of the Kuantan Club cricket team was the Kuantan Recreation Club (KRC) cricket team. During 1957–1960, there were many games played between the two clubs, sometimes on the small *padang* opposite the Police station next to the hospital, and sometimes on the main *padang* in front of the Law Courts. The games were serious and keenly fought. Although it was never mentioned, never even so much as put into words, there was a definite element of superiority tinged, I suspect, with what could be termed colonial prestige from the players of the Kuantan Club. This superiority did not go unnoticed by the KRC players. They responded to our slightly arrogant and worldly attitude by increased keenness, understandably, because they wanted to beat the hell out of us. The KRC players were mostly Indians. The Kuantan Club players were almost entirely Europeans. The KRC played attacking cricket, often with the bravado of young men facing impossible odds. They sometimes won the game, and that would be cause for an explosion of rejoicing and probably several beers and a great feeling of satisfaction. Stoic in defeat, we could hear the whoops of delight in the KRC building as we gathered up our gear to return to our club. Unfortunately, the players did not mix in the bar after the game. The KRC boys went into their own club building. We packed up our things and retired to our club.

Today the Kuantan Club is just a shadow of what it used to be. I appeal to the Town Planners to make absolutely sure that the Kuantan Club building is protected and looked after. Find and display as many of the photographs and memorabilia from the time of colonial Rule and turn it into a museum. That tiny corner of busy Kuantan could be turned into an instrument to teach modern Malaysian children how the Malaysians of 50 years ago fought for and strived for independence from the British. Use the Kuantan Club building as a museum to demonstrate for the Malaysian children the injustice of colonial rule, even if in certain circles there is a requirement to forget the past, or bury it in a sentiment of mild respect for some of the old colonial rulers.

It is true that many of the British expatriates had compassionate motives and a genuine interest in the future of the country. But it should be explained to the coming generations of Malaysians that colonialism was to the benefit of the British, even though in certain circles it is believed that the British seemingly practiced a benevolent form of colonial rule.

In those days when we played cricket, shade from trees around the cricket ground was important for the spectators. Both *padangs* were then richly planted with flame of the forest and jacaranda trees. The coolness and comfort of the shade attracted the youth of the district and other people interested in cricket as spectators, and they could spend a few relaxed hours under the trees around the *padang*, watching the game. The locals, often mostly those of Indian background, shouted keenly for their men to go for a quick run, or they applauded a good shot with the same enthusiasm of spectators at Lords or the Oval.

"Move your arse," Harry would petulantly shout at any of his own slow fielders. And, from the ring of spectators, Datuk A.A.S. Dobbie, the British planter and manager of Jabor Valley Estate, would shout his version of the Tamil expression, "*Voodya, voodya,*" if the batsmen hesitated to run. Mrs Windsor kept the score, with great concentration under a large sun hat, for the Kuantan Club and Mr Doraisamy, the State Veterinary Officer, did the same for the KRC. It was great fun, but it was intense and competitive cricket, and the gentle undertone of more serious conflict flavoured these games with special merit.

For the players and spectators from the Kuantan Club, lunch was arranged in the Club building and it was usually a curry tiffin. After a superb chicken curry and a torpor-inducing *gula malacca* served by Gin Lime, the head boy, the thought of going back out to the field was daunting. By 2:00 pm, the sun was at its fiercest point in the heavens, and the fielders and batsmen cast no shadows. For lunch, the KRC boys went back to their club house, which is now the Kuantan Tourist Association building. Hopefully, it is a protected building and part of Kuantan's historical heritage. I expect the KRC curry lunches were a good bit fiercer than those served up in the Kuantan Club. Although Gin Lime was a Hainanese, he could make excellent curries, and his Western cooking was just as good.

I have no hesitation in saying that a good Malay curry is among the best food in the world. The Malay language has its own word for food that is spicy-hot, which is *pedas*, as opposed to the word for heat in relation to temperature, *panas*. For example, beef *rendang* can be mild or *pedas*; in any event, if cooked well, it is a superbly composed dish of tasty ingredients. A mouthful is like a culinary journey, as each delightful taste assaults the tongue in minute explosions of ginger, cardamom, clove and cumin. A really good curry is the subtle mixture of the sharp, aromatic pungency of cardamom, the undertone of onion or shallot, and the tangy bite of chilli—just enough to enhance the flavour of the meat and bring out the excitement of a taste-burst of clove and ginger. Fish curry has a different composition of ingredients, often with the sharper flavours of lime, tamarind, lemon grass and spring onion.

Although I love a fish curry, to do justice to the splendid fish from Malaysian coastal waters they have to be sampled and experienced as the Chinese Malaysian cooks prepare them. Sea fish, freshly caught and served, steamed or fried, in a small Chinese restaurant, with a garnish of *kangkong belacan* and *ikan bilis*, and a dish of other local vegetables can number among the food delights of Asia.

For me, cricket was a lifesaver. It offered comradeship and an interest outside of planting topics. Planters used to be incredibly stuck on their profession. Whenever a group of planters sat around a table in the Kuantan Club, their conversation revolved around estate life.

"Well, Maurice, how are the elephants treating you up at Panching?" Bill Dobbie would be genuinely interested, as well as slightly spiteful. It concerned Dobbie's jealousy of the fact that Maurice's estate was being rapidly replanted, whilst his own Board of Directors were still reluctant to plough capital back into the company by replanting Jabor Valley Estate. The conversation among planters could be anything, from concern about elephant problems, the intricacies of *lalang* eradication, corrective fertilizer applications, the choice of cover crops, or the cost of drainage upkeep. The exchange of ideas was a way of keeping each other updated and such conversations, although they could be endlessly boring for non-planters, were a great forum for a young planter to learn his profession.

Although I had no opportunity to join in cricket practice during the week, I did manage to get away from the Estate to play on a Saturday afternoon or Sunday. I also played for the East Pahang Cricket Team. One of our first fixtures was sometime in May or June 1958, usually the hottest time of the year in Pahang. We journeyed to Temerloh, leaving Kuantan very early in the morning for a one-day match against West Pahang, their players came from Raub, Kuala Lipis and Bentong.

Just before lunch, we were fielding and I was bowling. I had already taken a couple of wickets, and, as any cricketer will tell you, a couple of wickets under your belt is exactly the prescription for extra effort. I was thundering along on my run-up and I think the ball was leaving my fingertips slightly faster than at any other time in my whole life. My pecker was up. When it was time to bowl my next over, Harry Wharton came up to me holding the ball and said:

"Listen, the Tengku Mahkota is going to knock a few balls, so for God's sake tone it down a bit. You know, take it a bit easy.

We need his interest in cricket." I noticed one of the batsmen walking away from the wicket back to the pavilion. The opposing Captain was walking towards the crease, deferentially escorting a tall, regal-looking Malay who was padded up and carrying a bat. I stayed next to the umpire, while the Tengku Mahkota took time in taking a guard of middle stump. "Tengku," called the umpire, "right arm over the wicket, six to come." Harry Wharton followed me back to the end of my run-up ,as I vigorously polished the ball on my trousers. "For Christ's sake Mike, slow it down and keep it short and outside the off-stump." I was very tempted to give that first ball everything I had, but I shortened my run slightly, and did as I was told. The ball kicked short on the dusty matting and went past the Tengku into the hands of the wicket keeper. But I could see from the way that the Tengku Mahkota shaped up to that ball that he had played some cricket before.

The next ball was a tiny bit slower and, as it deserved to be, it was hit to the offside past a couple of fielders. The Tengku Mahkota, the Sultan-to-be, had got off the mark and scored two runs. He stayed out on the field for a few more overs, and when he was reluctantly caught, but not off my bowling. He thanked us all and walked off, bat under his arm in a very professional manner. We all applauded him warmly and our match resumed. Since that time in Temerloh in 1958, I have been proud to say that I have played cricket with His Royal Highness, The Sultan of Pahang.

Girlfriend in England

When I left England for Malaya, I was in love with an English woman. She was a nurse. I was twenty, and she was twenty-seven. My parents accepted the relationship without reservation, although my mother did question me as to the difference in ages. "When you are sixty,"

she said, somewhat anxiously, "Joy will be approaching seventy."
Naturally, at such a young age I found the intervening 40 years to be
more that enough of a lifetime. "We love each other, Mother." I said
with a precocious finality. "And in any event, as you yourself have
said, age is purely relative." These words of wisdom I added, with the
disagreeable pompousness of youth intent on putting a concerned but
well-meaning parent into place. Joy's mother was adamantly against
the relationship. She suspected that her daughter's fondness for me
was misguided, and perhaps the result of having devoted her entire life
to nursing rather than using some of her time to search for a suitable
partner, a doctor for example.

Joy was a talented and wonderful nurse. When I first met her, I
was a patient and she was the Sister-in-charge of Ward 24 at Smallfield
Hospital near Horley in Surrey. Smallfield Hospital was part of The
Redhill Hospital Group, and its barrack-style wards were made famous
by pioneering plastic surgery performed on men and women with burn
injuries incurred during the Second World War.

On the ward, she was brisk and cheerful and superbly efficient, but
there was something about her manner, her face, her tall lithe figure that
gripped my heart. I fell in love with her with the intensity of youth.

Between bouts in hospital for surgery for an injured shoulder that
slipped in and out of joint, I made it my business to accomplish chance
meetings. I knew when she was working late, and I also knew that
the hospital bus would deliver her in the evening at 8:25 pm outside
the main hospital gate at Earlswood Common. If I stood by the tiny
pond at Meadvale, concealed somewhat by the hawthorn trees near the
small pond, I could surreptitiously watch for the bus to arrive. When
I saw the hospital bus swing into the car park, my heart would start
pounding and my breathing rate double. The arrival of the hospital
bus was my cue. As the bus turned into the main entrance, that was
the time for me to step gaily out in the direction of the hospital and

meet her, quite by chance of course, as she crossed the road. If she was not there, then I felt disappointment like a blow to the stomach. If she was there, then I would do my best to make everything about me appear calm and controlled, even though I had a feeling in my chest that seemed similar to the desperate fluttering of a trapped bird.

We started a relationship. The details of exactly how it all came about are only of interest to the two of us.

When I told her and my parents that I was considering taking a job in Malaya, Joy did not understand how I could possibly leave her behind in England and undertake a four-year tour of duty in Malaya under the terms of a contract that did not allow me to marry. "And for God's sake, why Malaya?" she demanded. Her brother had been killed in an ambush at Klian Intan, close to the border with Thailand, just six weeks after he joined the Malayan Police. After he was retrieved from the jungle by a patrol of British troops, he was first buried in a tiny cemetery in Kroh, but later his remains were transferred to the war cemetery in Taiping.

The promise of adventure, the desire to experience a different life, the conviction that one is somehow super-charged with special qualities are the young and untried self-assurances of a twenty-year-old who is led to the conviction that no problem could thwart his youthful enthusiasm. In my mind, I was quite certain that I would be able to find a solution to any of life's temporary problems. In short, I was pumped up by the arrogance of youthful inexperience—the same combination of feelings and emotion that pushes young men today to race their cars, in the middle of the night, on public roads at idiotically high speeds.

Shortly after my arrival in Malaya, just a few months into my contract, I was desperate with loneliness. Under a particularly heavy spell of desperation and anguish, and accompanied with a heavy heart and tortured mind, I sent Joy a letter, asking her to marry me. In the letter, I think I wrote that I would find some way to unravel *the complicated web that served to keep us apart. When I received her reply, telling me that she would marry me, my depression was changed to elation, punctuated with unbearable moments of missing her, of feeling that immeasurable young man's ache of not having her by my side. I even told Maurice Cotterill, my boss, and his wife, Sybil the news that I had become engaged (by post) to be married to the most wonderful English girl. And I remember how crestfallen I was when this universe-shaking news was met with raised eyebrows and questioning looks.*

I had served one year of my four-year contract when I sent Joy another letter. I asked her to release me from my promise to marry her. In the language of the day, I told her that I was a cad and a rotter and that she would be well-advised never to think of me again, as I was beyond redemption. It was the time when Ah Moi really entered my life. Joy sent me a telegram, saying that she was prepared to travel immediately and join me if I would only give her a sign. I cabled back that under no circumstances was she to even contemplate such action. I added that if she did come to Malaya to try to find me, then I would not be in the country to greet her. What bastards we can be.

CHAPTER 13

A Lift From The Sultan, With No Outriders

Early in 1959, I invested in a motorcar. In those days it was still appropriate to refer to motor driven vehicles as motorcars. It was a Vauxhall Wyvern, a four-cylinder box type car with the typical Vauxhall fluting down both sides of the bonnet. It was dark green. I would guess it was a 1947 model. I paid a few hundred dollars (this is before Malaysian currency was denominated in *ringgits*) and also had to trade in my beloved motorcycle, my delightful Triumph Tiger Cub. I purchased the car from Ah Heng, the same Chinese workshop owner who originally sold me the motorbike.

The car was the thrill of my life. It was the first car I had ever owned and I suppose, like all young men with their first car, it made me immensely proud. After riding the motorcycle in the rain and wind, I now appreciated the cover and protection of the car, not only from the rain but also from the onslaught of flying beetles seeking out the fascination of my motorcycle front lamp beam and smacking me full in the face.

Sometime in April or May 1959, when it was early evening and I was back in my bungalow after the day's work, I received a telephone call. The Irish accent of Brother Aloysius was unmistakeable, if somewhat agitated.

"Michael, you see we're in a spot of bother. We borrowed a jeep for the drive to Pekan, and on the way back, the thing broke down. So here we are stuck on the side of the road." He hesitated a few seconds, and then added, "Do you think you could come and pick us up?"

"Of course," I replied. "Where exactly are you?"

"Well I'm not too sure about that. But it must be about the twentieth milestone on the Pekan Road."

I quickly finished my tea, and explained to Ah Moi that I had to go and pick up a friend. Proudly climbing into the Vauxhall, I set off for the thirty-odd mile drive in the direction of Pekan, the Royal town of Pahang. By the time I arrived at the spot where Brother Al was patiently waiting alone, it was getting late and we greeted each other in the few minutes before it was totally dark. I remember seeing the last touches of light in the western sky before the darkness enveloped us in complete isolation on a very wild part of the road to Pekan.

"Well there's nothing else we can do," said Brother Al. "Turn your car round and we'll head back."

The Vauxhall was equipped with a gearshift attached to the steering wheel. Engaging reverse was sometimes a bit tricky. I drove in first gear a few yards past the spot where Brother Al was standing and found a place in the road that appeared to be wide enough to execute a classic three-point turn. I swung over the crown of the road to the edge of the drain, and engaged reverse for the full lock backwards manoeuvre. I executed this excellently and was ready to again engage first gear to swing me completely round in the direction facing Kuantan. The Vauxhall refused to slip out of reverse. The linkage was completely stuck. It was jammed solid. Whatever I did, clutched, double de-clutched, put the hand brake on, turned off the engine and tried again—the linkage would not budge. It had happened once before, but on that occasion I was able to get Ah Heng to come out to the Estate and fix it. He assured me then, that I would have no further problems.

"Don't worry Al," I said, desperately trying to keep my voice under control. I lifted the bonnet and asked Al to sit inside the car and fiddle with the gear lever. I reached into the mystery of the car's entirely dark insides and caught hold of the parts I felt to be moving. I tugged linkage levers, and pushed them and banged them but there was nothing I could do to release the linkage out of reverse gear. I guessed that the weight of the car, which was facing backwards down the camber of the road, was also not in my favour. My eyes searched the blackness under the hood, but there was so little light, that I could just have well worked with my eyes closed shut. I was covered in grease, literally up to my elbows.

"I am so sorry, Al. The car is stuck in reverse and there is nothing I can do to get it out." I was mortified. So, here was this kindly Roman Catholic teaching brother from St Thomas' School, who had trusted me to get him out of a tricky situation, and I had let him down. I was in a state of abject despair. I would readily have pushed my Vauxhall out into deep space if I could have done. We managed to find some stones to put under the wheels, just in case a few of the boys from the nearest kampong decided to play with it the next morning.

"Well, Michael, what shall we do now?" Brother Al was more disconsolate and resigned than I had ever heard him before. My maritime training told me not to leave the boat, or, in this case, the two broken-down vehicles. But, knowing just how isolated and how little traffic there was on that road, particularly at that time of the night, I reasoned it would be best to walk.

"Walk!" Exclaimed Brother Al," his bespectacled eyes shone huge in the light from my cigarette, "you must be joking." There was not the slightest trace of the usual smile on his face.

"I think there are some houses or a *kampung* about five or six miles up the road. And at least we will be moving in the right direction." I waited a few seconds, and then added, "We could wait here all night and not meet another car in either direction."

"Well, alright," he said. "I'll put myself in your hands." After my inefficiency with the car, I did not like the sound of that one little bit.

We started walking. I have never experienced such a dark night. The road was raised above a swamp, a low-lying area of poorly drained land with tall forest trees on either side. It was a perfect place for leopard, and I had heard several stories about leopards on the Pekan road. I had never read or heard an account of a leopard attacking men in a group, but I did not want to be the first. I missed the comfort of my walking stick, and we had absolutely no weapons. We walked in comparative silence; Brother Al, a ghostly creature floating along in his long white cassock, eerily visible in the intermittent cloudy starlight, and I, dressed in shorts and a short-sleeved shirt, nicely exposed to the mosquitoes that avidly sought out my bare skin. The darkness and the underlying fear fired my awareness to levels that can only be described as primeval. All my senses were vibrating like the strings of a soundless instrument. I quivered with fear and awareness. I am convinced I could have heard the lightest snap of a twig or the distant sucking sound of an animal's pad leaving the ooze.

At last, the lights of an approaching car appeared on the road behind us. We stood in to the side of the road and waved vigorously as it approached. It was a small car, built for four people and inside there were at least seven Chinese passengers. They all smiled and unnecessarily explained that the car was already full to capacity.

"Where you going?" the driver shouted, as if we were out on

an evening's constitutional amble. In my somewhat testy mood, I felt like telling him to mind his own damned business, but Brother Al calmly explained that we were on our way to Kuantan. When they heard this, they all exclaimed "Kuantan!", dissolved into shrieks of helpless laughter and drove on.

Low in spirit, we trudged on. We took heart and some comfort from the disappearing tail-lights of the car, but at the same time we were dismayed as the receding red flicker indicated a road that just went on and on. We continued to march into the darkness along the straightness of the road ahead without so much as the glimmer of even a small oil lamp ahead of us.

After perhaps another quarter of an hour of walking, our spirits were again lifted by the sight of distant headlights of another car, also approaching us from behind. It seemed to be a powerful vehicle travelling fast. We again positioned ourselves on the side of the road and waved and jumped up and down in the powerful beams of the fast-approaching headlights. The car did not even slow up but zoomed past us. My disappointment was tangible in the form of unkind words, despite Brother Al's presence. However, 200 yards down the road the car pulled up. We both ran towards the tail-lights. When we reached the car, I looked in at the driver. He was a Malay, equipped with a very fine with a *songkok* (Malay cap), and he was dressed in uniform.

"*Ma'af Inche. Boleh tolong bawa kita sampai Kuantan?*" I asked in my poor Malay. "Excuse me. Could you give us a lift to Kuantan?"

"*Kereta ini, ada lah, kereta Tuanku.* This is the Sultan's car." the driver replied

I peered into the back of the car and discerned the figure of His Royal Highness, Sultan Abu Bakar, Sultan of Pahang.

He leaned forward in his seat to look out at us and asked simply, *"Apa Sallah?* What is wrong?"

"I am so sorry sir," I said in English. Suddenly remembering that I had heard that he refused to speak to Europeans who had been in the country for more than six months in any language other than Malay, I continued in Malay. *"Ma'af Tuanku. Kreta saya suda rosak. Ta'boleh pakai.* My car has broken down. It can't be used."

"Naik, naik, naik kreta," commanded the Sultan, and waved us into his car.

Brother Al sat next to the Sultan on the back seat. I sat on a jump seat facing His Royal Highness. He insisted on shaking hands. I tried to explain that I was grease up to my elbows, although I had wiped the worst away with grass from the roadside. *"Ta' apa,"* said the Sultan graciously. "That doesn't matter."

He asked me questions; Who was I? Which estate did I come from? Who was my manager? He turned to question Brother Al, who had lived in Kuantan many years, but to my surprise, could speak little or no Malay, so I translated. But it was obvious that His Royal Highness spoke perfectly good English.

He gave us to understand that he was travelling to Kuantan to open the Cathay cinema. Therefore, the exact date of this incident can be determined if there are any records of that particular event. The Cathay cinema building is still in Bukit Ubi Road; however, now it appears to be in use as a furniture store, but not as a cinema. The whole building and the surrounding area are probably under threat and may soon be pulled down to make way for a new mega mall, or a new parking complex.

The Sultan insisted on the driver taking us exactly where we wanted to be let out. I thought it might be inappropriate, and also take him out of his way, to ask to be dropped off at the Kuantan Club.

"*Mercantile Benk, terimah kasseh Tuanku.*" As we climbed out of the car, the Sultan again shook hands with us and wished us well.

So, Brother Al and I knocked on the door of the flat above the bank, where Bill Dishington lived. We cleaned up in the bathroom, gratefully accepted a glass of beer and told Bill our story. Brother Al walked from the bank, which is now the HSBC bank on the same site, to his quarters at the St Thomas school. Bill Dishington kindly drove me all the way back to Sungai Talam Estate.

It is incredible to recall that in 1957, the Ruler of the State of Pahang travelled in a single car with a driver all the way from Pekan to Kuantan. He was not accompanied by police motor-cycle outriders and he was not surrounded by State dignitaries. Today, it would seem that if any of the Royal family move outside their residences, they are accompanied by flashing lights and wailing sirens, and the vehicles of ordinary road users are required to drive off the road and allow the cortege of vehicles to pass.

A few days later, and with the assistance of Mr Sidek, I wrote a letter of thanks to His Royal Highness. In my letter, we called on part of the phrasing of a Malay *pantun*, a section readily recognisable to any Malay. "*Hutang emas boleh di bayar, Hutang budi di bawa ke mati.*" Which, very poorly translated, means, debts of money or gold can be paid; debts of kindness follow one to the grave.

A year later, when I attended the Sultan's birthday celebrations the following April in Pekan, it was customary for all the guests to be received by His Royal Highness and Her Royal Highness the Sultana. I bowed to Her Royal Highness, and, being a man I was totally ignored. I turned and bowed to The Sultan. I said my name and said I came from Sungai Talam Estate. He smiled back at me, leaned forward to shake hands, and he asked, "*Tuan sudah tukar kreta?* Have you changed your car?"

"*Belum laggi, Tuanku. Ada la, di-belakan Istana.* Not yet Your Royal Highness. It's parked behind the Palace."

CHAPTER 14

West Meets East

In a sense, we are entirely locked inside our own minds, and we see and experience everything that happens to us, only through our own eyes. This colours our perception not only of the world, but of our understanding of everything that goes on around us. When someone, even a close relative, says something to us, we understand that message only when it has been filtered through our own complicated set of prejudices and our inherent need to translate messages in the way we want them to be, rather than the way they are. The process is exacerbated when looking back in time to past events.

A man, who became a friend of mine was a government servant employed in the Drainage and Irrigation Department. He arrived in Kuantan from Wolverhampton with his young English bride of only a few weeks. In England she had been a teacher. In Malaya, it was difficult for her to obtain a job, at least one that would pay her sufficiently to make it worth her while. Apparently they were a charming young couple, but the wife, Rosemary, soon gathered a reputation for being outspoken and indeed, somewhat critical of the way in which most European women spent—or wasted their time, as Rosemary was reported to have said.

Hugh and Rosemary were well-informed, sensible English people and they settled in a government house of simple standard somewhere near the Telok Sisek road in Kuantan. I must say here and now that I am forced to disguise names and places. Perhaps I should also mention that my recollection of events could be the truth as perceived through my recollection, after being filtered through years of my own memory. Bear in mind what I said about our own, often fallacious, interpretation of events. For the sake of this story I shall call my friend from Wolverhampton Hugh Taylor.

Sometime in 1958, the Kuantan water supply proved inadequate from sources in the Bukit Goh reserve. A pump house was built on the bank of the Kuantan River close to the northern boundary of Sungai Talam Estate. I became friendly with two of the young engineers involved in the project. They travelled frequently through the estate on their way to the river, and I would stop and talk to them for a few minutes if I met them when I was on my rounds. One of these engineers was Chinese and he came from Ipoh, the other was the young man from Wolverhampton, Hugh Taylor.

Six months after Hugh arrived, his wife left to go back to Wolverhampton.

"It got to the stage," he told me, "that I could not even take harmless magazines or even newspapers home. She accused me of looking at the pictures of women.

"What do you mean?" I asked. We were having a glass of beer in his bungalow, the bungalow that his wife had tearfully vacated in order to return to England.

"Well, for one thing, she thought I was looking lustfully at every female, including the pictures in magazines."

"Were you? I asked. He just looked at me with a half-raised eyebrow and an expression on his face that told me not to be stupid.

"Well, of course I look at attractive women. What man doesn't?" He put on a long-playing record with the title, 'The Panic is On.'

"Well, there were other things. She was not happy here.

Malaya is not easy for a young English wife, without transport. You see, I needed the car for my job." He continued in his deliberate, quiet way, an almost lazy way of speaking that disguised a restrained but explosive energy. "She did not particularly enjoy coffee mornings and the social chit-chat with the other *mems*. She found it very empty, very much a waste of time." With no warning, he jumped out of his chair and turned the record player off. "Come on," he said. "I don't want to talk about it. Let's go to the club for dinner. I'm hungry."

When Hugh's wife left, he and I spent a great deal of time together. He, an enforced bachelor with unaccustomed time on his hands, and me, a young man delighted with the comradeship of an older, wiser countryman. During the evenings we were together ,we searched out the company of other bachelors, visited the Police Officers Mess at Alor Akar, or ended the night with a *mah mee* or a *mee goreng* in the market place in Kuantan, stamping our feet at the rats.

Diving for Bailey-Bridge Sections

Today, there are three magnificent bridges over the Kuantan River. The first original bridge that was built to replace the the old wire ferry, is situated at the approach to the town on the road to the Kuantan Airport and Kuala Lumpur. Today, there is a second bridge constructed alongside the first, and there is a third new bridge built further down stream, leading traffic to Pekan and the South.

In 1958, the only way to cross the Kuantan River was by a ferry. To make the crossing, the first six or so cars would drive down a concrete ramp and drive across a ramp on to the ferry. The ferry driver operated a winch, which pulled the vessel over the river by a system of guide wires or cables. Sometime during that year, a PWD lorry was crossing the river on the ferry. Either the vehicle's brakes failed, the handbrake was not properly on, or the ferry was slewed round by a log in the river. Whatever the cause of the accident, it resulted in the lorry sliding off the ferry in the middle of the river. The lorry and a full load of Bailey-Bridge sections disappeared mid-stream into the muddy waters of the Kuantan River.

The PWD Engineer, in charge of roads and bridges and all the other civil engineering projects in the Kuantan District was a Canadian by the name of Chuck Bullock. He was a dashingly fit forty-year-old, with a pointed grey beard and an eye for the ladies.

On the day when the lorry disappeared into the river, my friend, Hugh Taylor of the Drainage and Irrigation Department, telephoned me at Sungai Talam Estate to ask if I would like to help him and Chuck Bullock salvage Bailey-Bridge sections out of the river. It sounded like fun. I took my swimming costume with me that afternoon and met the two engineers on the bank of the river. The time chosen was when the river was at its lowest, just before the tide turned and started pushing the waters of the South China Sea back up the of the river. Another ferry had been tracked out on the wire to the spot where the lorry had disappeared overboard. The three of us took it in turns to dive down and fasten metal hooks attached to strops to the individual metal sections of bridge. When we were clear of the water a group of PWD labourers, who were having a great time together with us on the ferry, hauled each section up on to the ferry by hand.

We continued the diving operation until we considered it wise to stop because of the fading light, even though most of the underwater work was done in comparative darkness because of the muddy water. However, we had recovered at least half the sections and felt justifiably good about that. We retired to Chuck's house for a shower and some beers and he stood us a dinner in the Kuantan Club. He said it was a grateful State Government's acknowledgement and thanks for our efforts.

Two weeks later, in the early evening, I visited a Telecommunications

Engineer by the name of John Gold. His house was on the bank of the river, not far from the hospital. We were drinking a beer and looking down into the swirling waters of the river. Suddenly, he grabbed my arm and cautioned me to follow him quietly. We crept down through his garden and closer to the bank of the river and looked over the edge onto a small undercut section of muddy flat on which a crocodile was crouching. He was difficult to see at first, as he was absolutely identical in colouring to the wet muddy background he was resting on. From his ledge the crocodile appeared to be watching the river. In the evening light, it was not easy to make out where he was resting, and if Gold had not known of his habits, I doubt if I would ever have seen him. He was at least twice as long as I am tall. He was enormous, and we watched him suddenly respond to some hidden message from the river, or, perhaps, his awareness of us, and slide effortlessly and without a splash into the darkening waters.

We tried to keep sight of him in the river until he submerged. I was surprised at his agility in the river. He moved fast and effortlessly with frightening speed before he disappeared. When I returned to my drink I quietened my troubled thoughts by assuming that the noise we had made when the three of us had been diving in the salvage operation would have kept him away from our diving operations. Perhaps, the metallic underwater sounds of bridge sections scraping against each other would have frightened him. But there is no doubt he would have known what was going on. It was a good thing we restricted our swimming close to the salvage ferry and were not tempted to take a relaxing swing up or down the river. Furthermore, where there is one crocodile of that size, there will be others. I imagine that his mate and their offspring probably patrolled the other side of the river.

Shortly after my crocodile visit to John Gold, the Telecoms Engineer, I heard that he was asked to leave the country within 24 hours, which is a polite way of saying that he was declared persona non-grata and kicked out by the government. It was said that he had insulted a Malay colleague's wife in public. He had apparently referred to her as being fat. I remember him as an intelligent and sober person, but he was outspoken. At that time in Pahang, Malays particularly, were sensitive perhaps even super sensitive to criticism. This was very understandable, as there were many instances of British and other expatriate officers who proved incapable of making a smooth transition from being colonial masters to the role of being a colleague on an equal footing.

In 1958, Malaya was proudly independent, and some Malay officials were more than alert to what they considered to be supercilious remarks. Although most Europeans managed the transition, some had difficulty, and they either resigned or were quickly kicked out. However, Malaya showed great maturity in acknowledging the worth of European Government servants, commercial employees and planters. A phased Malayanisation schedule was implemented so that Malaysians could themselves, in time, achieve the expertise needed to successfully take over.

CHAPTER 15

Transfer To Nada

About two and a half years into my four-year contract I was transferred from Sungai Talam Estate to Nada Division. Nada is at Kolek, just east of Sungai Lembing. In 1959, it was a very wild and isolated plantation; a place of hills and old rubber surrounded by the jungle. The estate was divided into two separate sections, Charu and Ampang. The Charu fields were hilly and eroded and planted up with non-selected seedlings that had been planted pre-1920. The renewed bark on the tapping panels was so scarred and difficult to tap that the trees were reaching the end of their commercial life. I seem to recall that the annual yield in terms of pounds of dry rubber per acre was down to less than 300 pounds.

The Ampang fields were flat, awful places to walk into. The whole overgrown area was infested with mosquitoes, and estate upkeep, had for several years been neglected, as the some of the fields had been taken out of tapping due to poor rubber prices and marginal yields. Good weed control on rubber estates has always been what is termed selective, removing the competitive and harmful plants and leaving the beneficial plants. This was usually achieved by employing a gang of labourers using *changkuls*, or the careful spraying of herbicides. This sort of husbandry was out of the question in the Ampang flats, where the only answer to the wild undergrowth was to attempt to drive a Massey Ferguson tractor between the tree rows with a brush cutter hitched to the hydraulics. The area was almost impenetrable; it was overgrown with siam weed, thorny lantana, Straits rhododendron, bracken and a variety of wild coffee.

Sometimes, when I ventured into the Ampang flats, I lit a couple of the thin 2-cent Indian-made *cheroots* at the same time, not for the pleasure of a rough, throat-searing smoke (they were strong enough to make my head spin), but in an attempt to generate enough smoke to discourage all but the most determined of mosquitoes from tearing me to pieces. I also picked lantana flowers, rubbed them together in my hands and then smoothed the juice and the crushed flowers on to any exposed skin. This seemed to help. With lime juice on my legs and boots and lantana juice on the rest of me I thought I smelt quite fetching in a musty, peppery way. The Malay name for lantana is *tai ayam*, which translates as chicken shit, because this is what the flower resembles.

The fields had an abundant supply of wild life, and the Ampang fields were a part of the estate that I never visited without my dogs or my walking stick. I cruelly worked on the theory that if I did surprise a leopard or a tiger, or a wild boar went for me the dogs would give me some warning, even if it were only their screams from the mouth of an animal. On several occasions I listened to the dogs' feverish, high-pitched yelps and found it wise to either stand my ground or turn and quickly retrace my footsteps. Barney was adept at finding his own way home.

Where the overgrown rubber trees met the jungle proper, in Ampang it was an area of poorly drained land with swampy growth. There were monitor lizards, big enough to be quite frightening, snakes, all manner of birds, rats, snuffling families of wild pig, the occasional tapir and sometimes even a scaly ant eater. Not that these animals were just waiting to spring out of their lairs and leap on top of me, but they were there, and, in such places, my senses moved automatically to a higher level of alertness.

I always thought of Nada as a grim and terrible place. The lines, where our labour force lived, were in a shocking state of disrepair, and at Ampang they were semi-detached units built up on stilts because the November and December rains flooded the area. My bungalow was a vast, ugly, poorly maintained cream-coloured timber building with brown trim. In the strictest terms it was not a bungalow in the English sense of the word, as it had two storeys. However, it was always called the Nada bungalow, never referred to as a house. At ground level the bungalow comprised of a cavernous dining room with a concrete floor rendered to resemble tiles. A dark polished dining table and four chairs were placed forlornly in the middle of the cave, and there was only an ageing group of rattan chairs for visitors to sit. My own lounge was upstairs, together with the two bedrooms, one on either side of the lounge. The kitchen, the *dapor* as it was called, was at the back of the house together with the servant's quarters and a storeroom. The generator was housed in a separate out-building slightly down the hill at the back of the bungalow to minimise the incessant noise of the Lister diesel engine.

The Nada bungalow hill was about half a mile from the office and the nearest staff houses and labourers' lines. It was entirely isolated from human contact and surrounded by rubber trees, the trunks of which were caked in oxidised and blackened spilt latex. At Nada I could have been murdered in my bed or held a honky-tonk party without the rest of the world having the remotest idea. In fact, I was once approached by a police officer and asked if I would allow him to invite some guests to use my bungalow for a blue film show. I politely declined, the Boy Scout code and Reigate Grammar School rescuing me once again. The garden surrounding the bungalow was ringed-in by a poorly-maintained barbed-wire fence and the ancient rubber trees were planted right up to the edge of the garden. In some places where root disease or termites had toppled the trees and opened up a view, I could see across acres of rubber and in the far distance make out the hills beyond Sungai Lembing and the mauve and lavender outline of the mountains in the vicinity of Gunong Tapis.

Nada was a far lonelier place than Sungai Talam. It was beautiful in a wild, unkempt way; so close to the jungle and so far from civilisation, it was rugged and disorderly, a place where nature had again taken over from the original tidiness of a planted estate. In spite of the 1926 floods, which decimated much of the wildlife in Pahang, the area around Nada teemed with animals and snakes. Elephants, tigers, leopards and wild pig abounded on the estate and in the surrounding smallholdings and jungle. From Nada, if you travelled in the right direction you would be able to stay in the jungle until you reached the Thai border and beyond; two, perhaps three or four hundred miles of primary forest or jungle. On one occasion I shot and killed a black and white tapir, which had unfortunately become trapped in a pig snare. I shot it to put it out of its agony, and that, to me, was a considered and deliberate act of mercy. But by shooting the animal I took on my shoulders a difficult problem with the Game Department.

I found myself missing my old bungalow at Sungai Talam, and missing too, the open fields of replanted rubber, which at the very least presented vistas that helped to lift one's eyes and expand one's hopes. I missed my friends, the close availability of cricket fixtures and the contact of the Kuantan Club. I also missed the ocean; that wonderful stretch of pristine beach at Telok Cempedak where I could swim and really feel the glory of youth and longing in my body, engulfed in the never ending cycle of wave and rough sand at the water's edge.

At Nada, I was shut in by dark, overgrown fields of old trees festooned with epiphytes; the only open land was swamp, or the valley of a river. The jungle around the estate was dark and foreboding and I only ventured in for special reasons. Nada Estate itself was like the surrounding jungle, full of leeches, and most days when I set off in the early mornings I soaped my field boots or squeezed the juice of fresh limes onto my legs to keep the leeches off me. To wear shorts is a good idea, as one can occasionally stop and examine one's legs to see if any leeches have started the journey in search of thin skin and the closeness of blood. On some occasions I would unlace my field boots when I returned to the bungalow for breakfast and discover leeches attached to the soft skin at the top of my feet, between my toes and on the inside of my ankles. Often they would drop off when filled with blood, but remain trapped inside the boot where I would squash them whilst walking. Sometimes my boots would be soaked with blood. But as I always had to walk in dew-soaked long grass or cross drains or rivers, my feet were usually wet and I thought the squelching, sucking feeling of wet boots was just water.

After some years, one becomes wiser and develops a sense of the geography of the tropics, a sort of second sense where the body instinctively reacts to the trees and bushes leeches seem to prefer. They frequent certain places; they seem to like the wild cinnamon plant, and when they breed they leave their egg-slime on selected trees. When they have hatched out they stick together like lumps of tiny worms purchased for bait, in bunches of hundreds, waving their suckers in the air in search of passing prey. In such places, one learns to automatically stop every so often to examine legs and arms, and take an occasional peep inside one's trousers. If a leech is travelling along on the skin, it is easy to pick it up and roll it between the thumb and forefinger before it gets the chance to attach.

I have been concerned about the stories of leeches that travel up your thigh and end up inside the urethra. I was also mildly fascinated but horrified of accounts of leeches invading the vagina of the women who work in paddy fields. When a leech does attach itself to the skin and has started the process of extracting blood it usually takes place without any pain, not even a slight sting, at least from the ordinary field leech.

However, there are other types of leeches. One variety that is particularly nasty is the striped buffalo leech, the *lintah*. This is a different sort of leech, much larger, with a sucking mouth powerful enough to attach to the thick neck-hide of a water buffalo or to ordinary cattle or wild pigs.

When removing the ordinary field leeches if they have started sucking blood, it is wise to gently pull them off your skin so as not to leave any of the leech's mouth in the wound. Strangely, when the leech has been removed an intensive itch develops and the puncture continues to bleed because of the anti-coagulant secretion the leech injects into the wound. The itching is awful, and the compulsion to scratch is the reason for subsequent infection, because it is almost impossible to not tear away with your fingernails at the punctured skin for short-term relief. Ordinary, old-fashioned tincture of iodine is the best remedy, as when applied to a fresh bite it seems to stop the itching and prevent infection.

At Nada I also had my own small diesel generator, which supplied enough electric power to light the bungalow, the kitchen and one bulb in the servant's quarters. If Ah Moi used the electric iron, to iron clothes, the load governor on the generator went wild and the engine would start surging followed by severe dips in power when the lights died away. The senior staff houses at Nada Estate were not supplied with electricity. The few shop houses, situated close to the railway line between Pasir Kemudi and Sungai Lembing, and the labourers' lines were also entirely without electricity. For lighting, each house managed at night with a small kerosene lamp that supplied enough light to do household tasks, but hardly enough light to read by. Even so, school lessons were learnt and many children of that generation succeeded by hard work and study to literally claw their way out of the estate labourer cycle and get an education. Some of the poorer families on Nada Estate fashioned lamps from old Brylcreem jars with a wick arrangement inserted through the screw on cap. I also think that a mixture of kerosene and diesel fuel was used in the lamps as it was cheaper, but it gave off a smoky flame. The shopkeepers would hang up pressure-operated carbide lamps that hissingly produced an intense greenish-white light beaming out into the road and illuminating the shop's wares of sacks of rice, chillies, shallots and onions and plastic and tin utensils and tins of condensed milk. The greenish light reached out to the surrounding undergrowth, making oases of brightness in the dark Malayan night attracting insects and large, beautifully marked hawk-moths that fluttered to the ground.

At Nada I settled down to very humdrum and lonely life, with only occasional flashes of excitement. I was unable to share events that took place on the estate with anyone except Ah Moi, because there were no neighbours, no friends with whom I could really sit down and enjoy an evening's talk. George Wood, during his weekly visits was usually on the way to Sungai Lembing and therefore in a hurry. During those brief visits he was usually only in the mood to snap out instructions, comment on tapping standards or poor work relating to *lalang* eradication, or complaint of poor yields.

The staff behaved in a cagey and obsequious manner with me, wary of my overtures at friendship and informality because, of course, I was the boss. Just as I was programmed and conditioned as Assistant Manager to behave in accordance with an unwritten code, a vague notion of being a leader, of setting an example, of being a paragon of virtue, so were my staff members, just as programmed to accept their role in playing up to me as the boss. In some ways my relationship with the staff and the labourers was just a continuity of the traditional Malayan manager-worker relationship, coloured by class, cultural, religious and colonial differences. At that time, it was too early to make a change. And I know now that I was too young and immature to have the courage to initiate the improvements that were so enormously necessary.

In the plantation sense, life was exciting at Nada. There was always something happening, something out of the ordinary. We had frequent brushes with elephants; roads flooded; once a leopard was caught in an illegal pig trap, and during one fearful night one of our two smokehouses burnt down.

Working on the estate, producing our own ribbed smoked sheets and keeping on top of the office work took me the best part of the day. The boredom and loneliness hit me, sometimes with overpowering sadness, in the evenings when the office closed and I walked back up the hill to the bungalow followed by Barney, my dog. He went absolutely everywhere with me, if I left my desk in the office he would immediately get up and trot alongside me to the packing shed, to the stores or the shops where it was part of my duty to check that the goods were clearly priced.

If I sat down in the shade outside a shop to buy a cup of coffee or a cold drink kept in a shopkeeper's kerosene-operated refrigerator, Barney would flop down close by, ignoring the curled up lips and stiff exaggerated toughness of the local dogs. The local dogs would stand their ground for a few minutes to consider the chance of a pack attack but usually they backed off and withdrew to watch events.

Barney was streetwise and a formidable opponent. He had left at least one litter of puppies at Sungai Talam, and if a bitch was on heat in the lines he would stay away for days at a time. He only came home to get an ear patched or flop out in the cool shade of the bungalow floor. Strangely, when he was courting like that he did not want food. He would rest up for a few hours and then resolutely trot back into the front of the pack of pursuing males. Mating was a serious business for him and I scolded him mildly when he finally came home, chewed up, exhausted, full of ticks and as thin as any abandoned local dog.

At the end of the day when I arrived back at the bungalow, Ah Moi would make me a pot of tea, which I took upstairs to where there was a panoramic view of the West. I would lean my elbows on the verandah rail and watch the setting sun's fading light deftly illuminate the hills and mountains of central Pahang. The slanting evening rays of pink, silver, mauve and lavender washed over the landscape and underlined the utter silence of the bungalow. It was the time of the day for utter quiet; the noises of the daytime, the sounds of insects and birds were now calming in preparation for the coming of night. The night sounds were not yet ready to start up their sudden buzz of activity that was triggered off by the setting sun.

This was the time when I longed for home, imagining that if I travelled long enough and far enough past those magically-coloured mountains I would eventually reach England and my home. Fortunately, I had Ah Moi with me and she was as lonely as I was. I also had my old Vauxhall car, so I could get away. And I had my dogs. If these evenings promised to be too sad and painful I made myself do something and often took the dogs with me down to the Charu River where I walked upstream from the road bridge into the jungle in search of really clean water. If I stood in midstream for a few minutes tiny fish would nibble at my feet, and perhaps a golden oriole would perch nearby. When it was dark I would call the dogs to me and drive home to the bungalow on top of the hill illuminated by a coughing diesel generator. Driving up the back road, round bends, I would catch sight of my home through the trees, standing out like a ship at sea in the night, on an ocean of rubber trees and jungle.

The Tyson Cup

Brian Tyson was a mining engineer who was working at the Sungai Lembing tin mine in December 1941 when the Japanese invaded Malaya. Tyson was Acting No 2 at the mine because Gordon Fairmaid was on leave. Vincent Baker was then the permanent General Manager. He had actually travelled out from England to join the company as early as 1911. Towards the end of 1941, when the remaining civilians, planters and tin miners knew from reports that the Japanese were very close to the village at Sungai Lembing, Baker contacted the British Adviser in Pahang, who was stationed in Kuala Lipis, for instructions. Baker was told to flood the mine and destroy tanks of diesel fuel needed for the pumps. The locomotives were to be sabotaged and the petrol stocks for the cars and the other vehicles torched. He was also instructed to make everything inoperable so that the mine would not fall into the hands of the Japanese as a working enterprise. According to Nona Baker's book Paai Naa, *Baker confided to his sister that when he gave the instructions to stop the pumps and then destroy them, and let the lower shafts and levels of the mine fill with water, he felt that his whole life's work was gone.*

Vincent and Nona Baker decided that they would never surrender to the Japanese, nor would they run before them like scattered chickens in front of a dog. Nona Baker had her two Doberman dogs, animals, which meant a great deal to her, destroyed. They were shot before she and her brother entered the jungle to attempt to sit it out and wait for the British and their allies to overcome what they assumed was merely a temporary set back and kick out the Japanese. They were not alone in their conviction that the Japanese term of occupation would only be short-lived. Maurice Cotterill and Brian Tyson were supposed to form a 'stay-behind-the-Jap-lines party'. They were looking for a suitable place to set up a radio receiver and transmitter. Their contact with the outside world, once they were firmly established in the jungle, was to be a Sinhalese electrician at the mine, a Mr Fonseca. In her book, Nona Baker wrote: "Fonseca was loyal to the British cause."

Cotterill and Tyson were apparently directed by the leaders of the 'orang bukit', as the communist Chinese (Malayan Peoples' Anti-Japanese Army) were known as, to move from Pahang to a camp in Johore. I know nothing of how they made the journey, or for what reason it was decided that they would be more useful in Johore, but I imagine they must have marched through the jungle perhaps mostly at night, along paths and tracks that were well known to the communists.

During my time in Pahang, which was during 1957–1965, once a year the Kuantan Club played a one-day cricket match against the Sungai Lembing Club XI. The trophy was The Tyson Cup, a silver plated memorial cup that was engraved with Tyson's name and the dates of his birth and death. The cup was donated by The Pahang Consolidated Company Limited as a memorial to the man who lost his life in the jungle and who happened to be very fond of cricket.

The cup represents a detail of Pahang history. I am convinced that many people would like to see the cup in the museum at Sungai Lembing. If the cup is in the Kuantan Club, then I think it would be a wonderful idea to hand it over to the museum with a brief history of the cup and the background for its existence.

There were many hundreds of Chinese people who moved into the jungle. They cleared land, planted vegetables and received meagre supplies from relatives on the outside. They chose the jungle over being tortured, or risk suffering worse atrocities at the hands of the Japanese. Many thousands of Chinese Malayans died during the occupation. It is not known how many Europeans chose to stay in the jungle but on the East and West Coasts there must have been several dozen. Not all of them survived. Maurice Cotterill survived and acknowledged his debt to the MPAJA. Vincent Baker died in the jungle a heartbroken man; his sister Nona survived. Her book Paai Naa *is mentioned, and a section enlarged to poster size in the museum at Sungai Lembing.*

CHAPTER 16

Hit On The Head
By The Shopkeeper's Wife

I seem to recall that the shopkeeper in this incident had the Chinese name of Phua. His *sing* (Chinese clan, or surname) was Phua. I think his *meng* (given name) was Ah Kitt. He was a Hainanese. That is to say that his family, whether his grandparents or his parents, originally left the island of Hainan and travelled to Malaya in search of a better way of life. Like all *nanyang* Chinese (Chinese of the Southern Seas), his family story, the way in which forebears populated South East Asia, would make fascinating reading. However, Phua was a shopkeeper at Nada, and he is in this story because he was charging the labourers too much money for rice and other commodities.

It was one of those overpoweringly hot afternoons, and trying to work in the divisional office was mind numbing and immobilising. I was thinking of packing up for the day and going for a swim in the river when a small deputation of five or six Tamil labourers arrived outside the office. The senior Conductor, a Mr Varghese (one of the Malayali estate staff clan), a tall man with a quaintly babyish face with dimples, listened to their complaints. He shook his head from side to side in irritation and to signify that he had understood what they were saying and that they should now cease talking and give him the opportunity to explain the matter to me. But Tamils, once they are in full pursuit of a story, are reluctant to give up centre stage.

Varghese wound himself up to his full height and extended a warning hand to arrest the speaker in mid-breath.

"It seems, Sir, that the Chinese shopkeeper-man, Phua, is charging these fellows too much for rice and other commodities. Cheating them, they say." The Tamils turned their attention from Varghese and stared intently at me to catch any nuances of mood in my gestures. I began as impassively as I could.

"Ask them to explain exactly how they are being cheated," I replied. When Varghese translated my request there was a torrent of Tamil as all of them tried to speak excitedly at the same time, pleased at having awoken my interest. Eventually, one voice prevailed, one of the tappers, Krishnasamy, assumed the role of spokesman. He alternated between speaking Tamil to Mr Varghese and speaking in the Malay language to me.

"*Tuan, bilah kita beli barang; beras, minyak, atau bawang, atau apa apa, kita mintak towkay itu tulis harga di dalam buku-buku kita. Dia buat itu,*" he paused for a moment and searched my face to make sure I understood what he was saying. "*Itu dia buat,*" he continued, urgently. "*Tetapi harga yang dia tulis dalam buku kita, adah-la lain daripada harga dia sudah tulis di barang!*" I listened to Krishnasamy explain that when labourers purchased rice, cooking oil or onions, they requested credit and asked the shopkeeper to write the amount in their books. This he did, but according to the Tamil deputation, the shopkeeper wrote in the books amounts that were higher than the agreed price for the items, or the weight purchased.

"*Bagi saya tengu buku buku ini.* Let me see some of their books."

"*Ta-boleh, Tuan.* We can't do that Sir; if we owe him money, he keeps our books."

"Do you sign for each purchase?" I asked. Thomas translated into Tamil. It seemed that those who were able to write or add their signatures, signed, but others simply trusted the shopkeeper, or agreed the amount with an ink pad thumb-print. "Well, if you sign, surely you must read the amount written into your book and see how much it adds up to before you sign." This remark, when translated caused an outburst of excitement. According to Mr Varghese's translation it seems that everything was written in their credit books in Chinese, the Tamil labourers therefore were unable to read exactly how much they were signing for. "Why don't they pay for their *barang* in cash?" I demanded. They looked at each other sheepishly and admitted that each one of them was in debt, in some cases they were in debt for more than what they could hope to earn in three months. "*Barang kali, ada baik jikalau awak larri semua orang.* Maybe it's a good idea if you all abscond." I said, somewhat sarcastically.

"*Lari di mana Tuan*? Sir, where can we run to?"

I thought there would be no better time than the present to take action, and absolutely no advantage in putting off the confrontation with shopkeeper. My head was aching slightly from the noise of the Tamil conversations. So, with my dog trotting by my side, we all walked in the hot, four o' clock sun, past the stores building, past the packing shed and the tapioca garden, and on to the shop-houses situated close to the railway line.

Phua was asleep in the back of the shop when we arrived. His wife reluctantly called him. At the same time, she demonstrated her mistrust of the situation by speaking angrily in Hainanese to her husband, to herself and to the small child she carried on her hip. Phua came out from the back of the shop looking sleepy-eyed, but with his usual false grin of pleasure at seeing me. I explained exactly why we were there and asked him if he would care to comment. I instructed the labourers to wait outside the shop but close enough to hear what was going on.

These situations, when it was word against word, were

difficult and it was essential to keep an open mind. I knew that my labourers could very possibly have some sort of a grudge against Phua, and, perhaps they were putting pressure on him about prices in order to get back at him. There was also no doubt in my mind that Phua would inflate prices given the opportunity. I knew this, as part of my job was to see that all the shops operating on our estate property displayed the prices of the main food commodities; rice and other foodstuffs had to be clearly marked, and priced—not in Chinese, but in Arabic numerals. This was a requirement from the local Labour Office, and occasionally their officers were sent to visit the estate from time to time on inspection rounds. During these visits checks were made on the way in which we were keeping wage records, our EPF contributions, conditions of hygiene and also on the pricing of goods in the estate shops.

I did not like Phua. I never did. He was an oily merchant. Like the flour he sold, I found him weevilish; very mealy-mouthed to my face, but I am quite sure he called me a mother-fucker under his breath in Hainanese, as soon as my back was turned. The Chinese are world champions in the awful swearing stakes. The word, *tiu* or *teeyu* is constantly used among Chinese labouring classes and is the equivalent of the English swear word 'fuck'.

Having been woken from his afternoon sleep, Phua spent a lot of time flapping around me and explaining just how unreliable the Indian labourers were. He beseeched me to understand that over the years he had lost a great deal of money because labourers purchased goods from him and subsequently were unable to pay for them. He went on to explain that he would then be obliged to extend credit to them in the hope of recovering his bad debts. He had a point, of course, and no doubt he had run up some bad debts. However, I decided that I would send in a written report to the labour office in Kuantan and request them to send a Chinese-speaking officer to investigate my labourers' accusations. In the meantime, I confiscated six or seven of the credit books, which Phua held as his record of the labourers' transactions in his shop. To satisfy Phua I gave him a written receipt for the books, stating the date and reason for my confiscation.

I sent copies of the report to George Wood and when he questioned me about events I insisted that we process the complaint to the Labour Office. George was reluctant but eventually said, in his broad Scottish dialect, "Well, Michael, if you think it is the correct thing to do then you must just go ahead and do it. But I warn you, you will just be pulling a whole lot of extra work down on your head, and it's not at all sure that you will get a favourable result." He thought for a while, taking a cigarette out of his ever-present tin of fifty. "You might not get any result just make a lot of bad blood around the place. Remember, it's not everybody who is willing to have a shop at Nada. It's not as if they're going to get incredibly rich from selling a few katties of rice to the labour force."

I acknowledged that I understood what he was telling me and then added, "At least the labourers will see that we take their problems seriously, and that we are on their side if it comes to them being cheated by a lousy shopkeeper."

The case went forward to the Kuantan Labour Office and within a week two Labour Officers arrived on the estate, one was an Indian, a Tamil, and the other a Chinese. Some time towards the end of the month I received a letter from the Labour Office, with a copy to The Manager, Kuala Reman Rubber Estates, a copy to the National Union of Plantation Workers' representative on Nada Estate, and a copy to the shopkeeper himself, Phua Ah Kitt. Briefly, the letter stated that as a result of complaints from the labour force at Nada Esate, Division of Kuala Reman Rubber Estates, Ltd, Mr Phua Ah Kitt had been found guilty of dishonesty with the pricing and recording of prices in the labourers' credit books. As a result, his shop would be closed and his license to operate withdrawn. He had 30 days from the date of receipt to wind up his business.

I thought these were very tough measures and had only expected some form of reprimand. I did not expect the Labour Office to close him down with only 30 days' notice. The estate owned the building, for which he paid us a nominal rent of fifteen dollars a month, so at least he was not going to suffer more than relocation costs he was not faced with by having to sell the building.

At the end of the official letter there was a line requesting me to obtain the copy of the Trading license issued by the Labour Office, which by law should be displayed in his shop premises. This certificate was to be returned to the Labour Office in Kuantan.

That afternoon I received a telephone call on the landline from Panching, it was from George informing me that Bill Dobbie, Datuk A.A.S. Dobbie, JP wanted me to visit him in Kuantan. George informed me that Bill Dobbie had suggested that I might like to have breakfast with him in the Kuantan Club the following morning at 9:00 am. An invitation from Bill Dobbie was not an occasion that occurred often in my life, it was therefore more of a command than a polite request. I knew there would be a reason for him to want to meet me; this was not a breakfast invitation because he enjoyed my company. There would be something. And I was a little disappointed in George for not giving me more direction as to how I should approach the meeting. Dobbie was the Manager of Jabor Valley Estate and had been made a *datuk* by the Sultans of both Pahang and Terenganu (*datuk* is a title granted by the Sultan and in effect creates a local Chieftan, the British equivalent of being knighted).

Naturally, I asked George if he could tell me what this was all about. I wanted to know exactly why I was invited thirty-odd miles on an awful road to have breakfast with the most important Planter in the district.

"Well, it has to do with Phua and the shop. I think Bee Huat, the bus company *towkay*, has been talking to Bill Dobbie, and they are both of them *datuks*, you know."

"What about the shop," I demanded. My ridiculous pride manifesting itself as petulance in my suspicions of what seemed to me to be like the whiff of an attempt to interfere with The Labour Officers' just and correct, if somewhat severe, decision to close the shop down.

"Well, if I were you I would make the trip down to Kuantan and find out what he has to say." George said this with a certain air of finality, closing the topic for further discussion. "I'll send a driver and my Land Rover up for you. Will 8:00 am suit you?" I thanked him and we rang off.

The following morning, dressed in field gear, but wearing clean, well-pressed shorts, I jumped out of the Land Rover at the Kuantan Club some minutes before nine and waited for Bill Dobbie to turn up. At precisely 9:00 am, his dark-green Rover saloon car turned into the Club driveway and he parked in the covered garages immediately next to the rear entrance in a parking space reserved for the President of the Club. Dobbie was a large man in every possible way. When he wanted to be, he was immensely charming. He was always ready with a compliment and was obviously knowledgeable and well-educated. He spoke with a powerful deep voice in a cultivated but not affected

English, it was an elegant English and usually a joy to listen to, as he was brilliant at copying accents and an excellent mime. He was quite an actor.

He strode in briskly walking past the full-sized billiard table and made straight for his customary chair, which was at the table closest to the bar. The main entrance to the Club, and the library shelves were off to his right. From where he sat he could follow the events taking place outside on the road. He could look out of the window at passersby, particularly the women and the older girls on their way to the Methodist Girls' School. Malay women, in those days did cover their heads as they do today, they did not need to wear a scarf and the feminine and flattering *sarong* kebaya was fashionable.

"Good morning, Michael Thorp," he boomed, waving me to sit down in a chair on the opposite side of the glass-topped table. "Gin Lime," he shouted. But the Club's head boy and catering contractor was already waiting for him, and moved forward into Dobbie's line of sight. It was typical of Bill Dobbie, to clown. "Oh my God," he expostulated. "Don't do that," he held his hand to his heart, as if the shock of seeing Gin Lime appear like a genie out of a bottle was too much for him. Gin Lime laughed politely.

"*Selamat pagi, Tuan*." the Chinese contractor said with a respectful bow of his Brylcreemed head.

"Good morning Mr Lime. Can we? Well, that is to say, could we, may we, have some coffee?" The over-emphasised politeness made Gin Lime giggle.

"*Kopi, dua orang, Tuan.*" Dobbie then apparently remembered that I was part of his order for coffee and asked me,

"Coffee alright?"

"Yes please," I replied.

"*Baik lah*, well, don't just stand there," he said to Gin Lime,

Farewell party by staff of Jabor Valley Estate for Bill Dobbie, A.A.S. on his retirement, Moonlight Hotel, Kuantan. Bill Dobbie (standing) giving a thanksgiving speech.

with mock severity designed to amuse and entertain his audience of two.

"Sit, sit, sit, sit." I was commanded. I sat in the chair indicated and importantly placed my brief case on the chair next to me, within easy reach.

"Let me explain something," Dobbie said, in a very business-like manner. "I am not interested in interfering with any of the affairs that go on, on your division. I have already explained this to your manager." By choosing to use the words 'your manager', he very neatly put me into my inferior place. He established the ground rules by using the words, 'your manager'. He took it for granted that I would understand that decisions involving my division were made above my head, at managerial level. Perhaps George even discussed such managerial decisions with Dobbie. George might very well do that in deference to Dobbie's seniority in the district, and, after all, Dobbie was Chairman of The Pahang Planters' Association.

"Now, tell me what happened between you and that wretched shopkeeper," Dobbie commanded. I related events, how my labourers had turned up at the office at Nada and made serious allegations of being cheated by the Chinese shopkeeper. I went on to explain how I had responded and the action I had taken, and, eventually, how I had insisted the investigation had to be done by representatives of the Labour Office.

"And now, finally," I continued, "we have received a letter from the Labour Office to say that they are withdrawing Phua's license to operate the shop." I took the letter out of my briefcase and passed it over to Dobbie. "He has less than a month, now, to wind up his business," I said.

"Michael," said Dobbie, the subtle use of my first name elevated me to equal rank, at least for the duration of this conversation. His tone made me feel that he was bringing me into his confidence, and he leaned forward towards me slightly, "You see, I am a *datuk* and there are certain occasions such as State Council meetings where I meet other *datuks*." He stopped and sipped from his coffee. "For example, Datuk Phua of the Bee Huat bus company has had a word with me, you know, one *datuk* to another. And he has asked me to request you to please reconsider the charges against the shopkeeper at Nada, who also happens to be a relative of Datuk Phua." I started to reply that it was out of my hands.

"Now, Michael. Just let me finish what I have to say." He leaned back in his chair and studied some people who were walking past the window outside the Club on the street. "You see, Datuk Phua is a Hainanese; very proud people, these Hainanese, they are experts in catering and restaurants. Datuk Phua is a leader of the Hainanese people here in the Kuantan district, including Nada and Sungai Lembing. So he is willing to give me an assurance, you know the sort of thing, one *datuk* to another *datuk*, well, he assures me that he will personally make sure that this so called cheating, if it was cheating, will not happen again." Dobbie took his eyes away from the window and looked at me to gauge the effect his words were having on me. "I told Datuk Phua that you were a promising young man with a good future here in Pahang, a good planter, the sort of chap that was needed for the future of the industry and all that, and I promised him that I would have a word with you."

I felt very angry at the obvious interference in what I considered to be Nada business and I felt unsure of myself. Fortunately, I kept my mouth shut and did not blurt out the first ill-considered response that occurred to me. I leant back in my chair and tried desperately to control my body language and the trembling that I felt sure he would notice. I was appalled that Dobbie apparently was unable to understand that if I agreed to his course of action then he would be instrumental in my loss of integrity, not to mention, loss of face with my own labour force. If I were to give in, and say,

"By all means if we have Datuk Phua's assurance that the shopkeeper will, in future, be of good behaviour, then we can all give him another chance."

Needless to say, I did not think it was possible to just give in after having come so far. I felt that it would be entirely inappropriate to give in, for my own sake, and for the sake of the company and for the sake of the labourers. I wanted justice for the labourers, which meant that I wanted an example to be made of Phua, and I was sure that the Labour Office considered this affair to be an opportunity for them to also demonstrate that they actually did things, that they were incorruptible and that they too wanted to make an example of a dishonest shopkeeper.

"Shall we eat breakfast, while you think things through?" Dobbie said, magnanimously. "Is bacon and egg alright for you?" He was about to call for Gin Lime in order to give him the breakfast order, but I stood up and faced him across the table and very deliberately, I also picked up my brief case.

"Thank you for the invitation to have breakfast," I said, "but I grabbed a bite before I left Nada this morning." I tucked the brief case under my arm to make it perfectly clear that my intention was to leave.

"I hope you are not thinking of leaving," Dobbie said, his voice assuming a shade of menace. I chose to ignore the hostile signal and said, "While I am in Kuantan I am going to take the opportunity of getting a few things done for the estate, you know, a new hydraulic pump for the tractor, that sort of thing."

"Will you think about my request, and let me know." Dobbie's voice was coldly bland. It was clear that he was also having difficulty in keeping control. I could tell from previous experiences with him that he was on the point of shouting at me and commanding me to sit down, telling me that I could only leave when he said I could leave.

"I don't think there is anything for me to think about," I said with considerably more calm than I felt. "The decision was made by the Labour Office, and from their investigations the man has clearly been dishonest." Somewhat fussily I pushed my chair back exactly into position, to the inch, squarely in front of the table. "The man has been exploiting our labour force," I somewhat pompously added. "He deserves to get the push."

"Boy!" Dobbie called for Gin Lime, who again appeared almost immediately from behind the door at the back of the bar indicating that he had probably been listening to our conversation. I quite suddenly remembered that Gin Lime, like the shopkeeper and the bus *towkay*, Datuk Phua, was, of course, also Hainanese .

"Mr Lime, bacon and egg for one. The *Tuan* will not be joining us for breakfast." With that I was dismissed.

"Goodbye, Sir." I said. Dobbie just stared at me with a severe look of anger on his face. I nodded with a grim but polite smile and I walked out of the club.

When I returned to the estate, it was late in the afternoon and Ah Moi made me some tea. I was sitting, brooding about the events of the day when I heard the estate Bedford lorry grind its way up the hill, and I heard it turn into the garden and stop outside the front entrance. Doraisamy the driver, walked to the back of the bungalow where I heard him talking to Ah Moi. Eventually, she came up the stairs and said the driver wanted to talk to me. I went downstairs, slightly irritated at being disturbed in the bungalow, to find out what he wanted.

"*Ada barang, Tuan.* Your items are here, Sir."

"*Apa barang?* What items," I demanded.

"*Barang barang daridada Towkay Phua, Tuan.* Items from *Towkay* Phua."

I went out to the lorry to investigate. On the back of the lorry were two sacks of rice, small sacks of flour, a cardboard box containing tins of pilchards, numerous tins of imported biscuits, tins of kerosene, dozens of bottles of beer tied together in string packages of six and two live chickens still trussed to each other by the legs. Doraisamy opened the cab door and showed me the bottles of whisky and cognac that were not entrusted to the back of the lorry.

"What is all this?" I demanded.

"I don't know, Sir. Towkay Phua asked me to bring the lorry to his shop and then deliver all these things to you."

I was furious. I was furious to think that Phua would have the audacity and nerve to use my own lorry, and my own driver, to deliver a bribe to the bungalow. Was he completely thick? Did he not understand that everyone on the estate would now know that all this stuff had been delivered to my door? My first reaction was to jump up into the cab of the lorry and instruct Doraisamy to drive back down to Phua's shop, where I would then personally throw all the goods at the obsequious shopkeeper. Fortunately, the time I had spent in Malaya had served to teach me a little caution.

I instructed Doraisamy to call out the size or the quantity or the number of packages of each and every item, which I carefully noted on two pieces of paper. When we had a complete list and tally I wrote down the following sentence: "The above noted goods and items, which have not been ordered by me, and are hereby returned. I refuse to accept receipt of these goods, signed Michael Thorp. Witness S. Doraisamy, driver." I added the date and then signed the note, and instructed Doraisamy to sign as witness.

I then turned to Doraisamy and explained that he must return all the goods forthwith. In addition, he was to obtain Phua's signature as a receipt for the return of the goods.

"You are not allowed to leave his shop without his signature for receipt of those goods." I was unnecessarily angry with the driver, although none of this was his fault. "And another thing," I continued. "I shall be sending him a bill for the hire of the estate lorry and for overtime payment to you, the driver." Doraisamy's face broke into a worried smile, "*Baik, Tuan.*" He said to signify that he had understood.

"And another thing, Doraisamy, when you have that receipt bring it back here to me immediately. Is that understood?"

"*Baik, Tuan.*" He hesitated a moment with a questioning look on his face to see if I was going to say anything more and then swung himself back into the cab of the Bedford and reversed the lorry in front of the garage and drove off down the hill.

I waited a couple days for events and my own temper to quieten down and decided it was time to visit the shopkeeper in order to obtain the license for him to trade. I was following up on the request from the Labour Office. After my morning rounds I returned to the bungalow for a shower and change and ate my breakfast. I walked down through Charu Field 6, through terraces of old, gnarled rubber trees to the divisional office, a faded Cuprinol-green painted shack with a corrugated asbestos roof, a cement floor and three miserable desks.

The conductor, Mr Varghese was sitting at one of the desks working out individual crop figures for the tappers, as the end of the month was fast approaching.

"Mr Varghese, can you spare a few minutes. I want to walk up to the Chinese shop and I may need a witness."

"Certainly Sir." Varghese closed the books he was working on and joined me on the dusty road leading to the shops. There was a small clump of coconut trees at the road junction and a Tamil boy had climbed up to harvest some green nuts.

"Be careful, Sir," said Varghese as one coconut after another fell to the ground with a bruising thud and then skeetered like distorted bowling balls in different directions across the road.

We reached the shop house where I went in and asked Mrs Phua if her husband was home. She said in the surliest possible manner, her lips curled in unmistakable hate, "*Phua suda pergi Kuantan. Saya ta tahu bila dia balek.* Phua has gone to Kuantan.

I do not know when he will be back." I placed the letter I had received from the Labour Office on the counter in front of me and explained to her in Malay that the letter requested me to collect the license from the shop and send it to the Labour Office. I was looking down at the letter when she hit me. She hit me so hard on the head with a large piece of firewood that I staggered backwards away from her, which was a good thing or she would have hit me again. I had no warning, and I did not realise for a split second what had happened. Then the pain burst in, hammering into my brain. I looked up to see her holding the piece of wood in one hand. She realised that she was too far away to hit me again. I could see in the fleeting look of fear that having hit me she expected me to retaliate. I think she was surprised that I was still on my feet. Standing, I represented some considerable danger. She bent down to scoop up her child, an infant with just a shirt and no pants. She was ready to flee or fight, her child with her.

I was just immensely shocked at the pain. I was also amazed that she had done such a thing. Anger and rage surged through my body in a furious desire to hit back. I stormed forward, lunging at her and wrenched the piece of wood out of her hand. I continued to hold her arm and stood, threatening her with the piece of wood, teetering on the edge of actually hitting her with her own weapon. She did not flinch, but stood looking at me, her arm cruelly held in my left hand and twisted painfully round. With anger and hatred glaring from her eyes she spat at me, full in the face. I really hated her for that, and at the same time I admired her tremendously. She looked at me like a wild animal, her face completely defiant, her Chinese nostrils flaring, her nipples leaking milk into the material of her blouse. Giving her arm an additional spiteful twist, I let her go and stepped back out of range. I continued to hold the piece of wood in my right hand and, at that moment realised that I was giddy from the blow, and from the adrenalin pumping through my veins. I put my hand up to my head and felt the wet stickiness of blood oozing through a painful cut and lump in my scalp. Unfortunately, I tossed the piece of wood down on the floor in front of her. I regret that I did not take that piece of wood and keep it with me for the rest of my life to remind me of what bravery is, how it is possible to misuse power, and how humility and negotiation is far more important than confrontation and violence. She was wrong to hit me, but I admire the protective forces that were surging through her.

I drove to the Sungai Lembing hospital where the English doctor, Brendan Freeman inserted several stitches in my aching head. I was told to take it easy for a couple of days as I had a light concussion. I then called at the Sungai Lembing Police Station and made a Police report, where, I think, the Malay Police Constables had a couple of discreet laughs at my expense. Many times in the intervening years I have secretly admired that woman, Mrs Phua. She was fighting for her family and for her husband, fighting for their livelihood. To her, and indeed to her husband, I represented the officious, callous and arrogant colonial masters that Malayans generally would be happy to see leave.

Shortly after the blow to the head, I was transferred to Kuala Reman Estate, at Panching. George and the Visiting Agent explained that I was needed at Panching in order to help with the heavy replanting programme recently approved by the Board, in London. I accepted the fact that there was much more work to do at Panching than at Nada, but I have always suspected that there were other forces at work that led to my transfer. Perhaps it was the *datuk* grapevine insidiously making sure that a certain Junior Assistant Planter should have his arse kicked.

Perhaps it was influence and peer pressure brought to bear on my manager. Perhaps the Labour Office caved in when threatened with complaints to Kuala Lumpur at Ministerial level. Anyhow, subsequently there were a number of unexplained events. I heard that Phua had lodged an appeal, and that he was also willing, if necessary, to take his case into the courts. However, as George said with an expressive shrug in his inimitable Scottish way, "It's out of my hands, laddie."

I shall probably never know what really took place behind the scenes, between George, Datuk Phua and Datuk Dobbie, in order to have me moved away from Nada. To this day I am convinced that my transfer was organised in order to allow Phua, the shopkeeper, to remain on the estate in his miserable little shop down near the railway line. What I do know is that it was Phua who continued to run his shop at Nada, and it was me who had to pack up and leave. I have often wondered if the labourers at Nada, all those families with the falsified credit books, ever actually appreciated what I tried to do. They all knew I got hit on the head.

To get away, you bite your leg

On Nada Estate, wild pigs were caught in several ways. The most humane method was when the hunters erected a stoutly built cage constructed from timber stocks and saplings as thick as a grown man's thigh. The posts were banged well down into a soft piece of ground, very close to each other, so that there was no chance of a captured pig bashing or levering its way out. The hunters would choose a spot favoured by wild pig; a swamp, or close to a stream, or on a known pig run through the jungle and belukar. *The tops of the posts were stoutly lashed together with* rotan *strips for added strength and the diagonal supports were wired into place.*

An enormously heavy trap door would drop down and close off the cage making it impossible for the pig to retreat. The dropping mechanism, a cunning peg arranged with a connecting piece of wire, would be triggered off by a snuffling snout tempted into the trap to examine the bait of ubi kayu or yam planted or dug into the ground. If an animal was lured into the trap and just touched the bait, then the door collapsed shut and the animal would remain trapped until the hunters came to kill it with pig sticking spears and parangs.

The hunters were usually the Tamils who lived on the Estate, as the Malays do not eat pork. Tamils, at least the Tamils who lived on the estates in the 1950s ate the meat of wild boar; this was not strictly allowed for practising Hindus, but hunger often dictates behaviour. The Chinese at Nada certainly were fond of wild boar paying well for the meat, but they were not hunters in the same way that the Tamils were. The older Tamil hunters often sported elegant, waxed, toddy-drinker's moustaches, and when they were ready for hunting, they stripped down to a simple short loincloth and smeared coconut oil on their bodies for agility and good luck. If an animal had been trapped, then the hunters would arrive with long sharpened spears, which they stuck into the screaming captured animal until it was tapped of both blood and strength. The pig or other animal was then carried back to the lines hanging from a pole straddling the shoulders of two or more men. The dogs would occasionally jump up to lick at the blood that dripped from the kill. The hunters would shout 'haak' to scare off the dogs if they nipped at the dead animal's snout or ears.

One of the illegal methods, which I tried my best to eliminate from the estates where I worked, was the setting out of snares; infamously cruel wire nooses attached to a young bent over sapling so designed that when triggered the tree sapling sprang upright tightening the snare and capturing the pig in the wire noose by its leg or its neck. Usually, it was a leg. Sometimes an animal would be half lifted off the ground, remaining caught until the hunters arrived. The animal would constantly pull and tug with sickening desperate rushes for freedom, all the time tightening the wire, which would bite deeper and deeper into the flesh until it cut into the bone.

Sometimes the hunters took their dogs and would position a couple of men with buckets to bang at an appropriate point, and then, working around the swamps and belukar in a long curve, the hunting party would drive the pigs towards the hunters with spears. Dirty thin mongrels yapping excitedly followed by black, oily men with long spears listening intently for the snuffle of pig or the sound of crackling undergrowth. Frequently, a dog would get ripped and bitten to pieces by a boar standing his ground in the face of the beaters and their chivvying dogs giving his sows and their litter's time to get away.

Evening was a good time to hunt for wild boar. It was the time just before the darkness folds down like a wrap thrown over the jungle. During the day the pig have been laid up in the swamps in their impenetrable lairs, and, at night, there were usually no people out in the estate, so it was relatively safe for the boars, the sows and the young to come out and forage for food.

On one occasion, on the edge of Field Charu 7, right up against the jungle boundary in a dark part of the estate, someone had set a pig snare and, instead of a pig, a black leopard had got itself caught by its left forepaw in the thick metal wire noose. It was a beautiful strong male, his underlay of spots only visible when you were very close to him. If a tiger or leopard was accidentally caught in one of these pig snares or traps the perpetrators chose to keep quiet about the tragedy and they would just leave the animal to its fate. Which meant that it would inevitably die, a lingering awful death, of pain, dehydration and starvation.

I was told about this incident one afternoon when a mandor, Subramanium, came into the divisional office and reported that there was a big cat caught in a pig snare. He said that he thought it was a leopard and that it had been in the snare for several days. He mentioned that it was in Field Charu 7, an area of ancient rubber trees that had been taken out of tapping to rest, so there had been no reason for anyone to visit that part of the estate, particularly as it was right out at the edge of the jungle. "How did you get to hear about this?" I asked.

"Well, Tuan. I just heard somebody say something, when we were weighing in the latex this afternoon." He raised his shoulders and stretched out his hands towards me before continuing. "I don't know who mentioned it, I just heard it." I knew better than to ask any further questions. This was exactly the sort of situation where one just accepted things. I knew if I pushed Subramanium for names, then, in the future, I would never get any information from him about anything.

We decided that it was best that we should visit the area. If the animal proved to be still alive it would be a great danger to anyone who approached. If the leopard escaped, it would in all probability be terribly injured and possibly die a lingering death. However, if the leopard escaped and survived its wounds, it could possibly turn into a man-eater, or attack domestic cattle or goats.

I summoned the estate watchman and took some heavy calibre cartridges out of the safe in the office and handed them over to him. I remember it as a distinctly hot afternoon. At 3:00 pm, the Malaysian sun beats down in merciless waves of heat that it is wise to avoid. I took my dogs back to the bungalow, where they were highly insulted to be tied up to one of the pillars downstairs.

They were whining disapproval when I drove off, but I did not want either of them to be attacked or sideswiped by a leopard's paw. I told Ah Moi to release them after half an hour; it was usually enough time for them to decide not to follow after the Land Rover but to stay at home and wait for my return, particularly if she gave them some food.

We parked the Land Rover at the side of the main road that carried the sporadic traffic between Panching and Sungai Lembing and walked up the hill path leading to the field and estate boundary. After a 10-minute walk, when we were a couple of hundred yards from the spot where Subramanium told us the leopard was trapped, we paused to size up at the terrain and map out our strategy. I felt sure that the watchman was a better shot with his shotgun than I was, and I certainly think he was more confident. We decided that he should approach as close as possible, and, when he had a clear shot at the animal, he should go ahead and put it out of its misery. Neither I, nor Subramanium had guns, although I had my parang *with me, a long locally produced knife for slashing undergrowth. Subramanium never went to the field without his* parang, *but it had the form of a meat chopper, at least my parang had something of a sharp point. It was agreed that Subramanium and I should follow a few yards behind the watchman, one on either side of him. We inched forward under the shade of the old rubber trees trying to peer over the top of the interrow undergrowth that badly needed slashing.*

The jungle exudes a feeling of menace that can engulf with an intensity reaching back into our past. Primitive fear. It is something to do with the smell. It is the darkness, the hostility of ripping thorns and slippery roots making a footing difficult. It is the immediate realisation that the animals have the advantage. This fear, this feeling, this ancestral awakening promotes a quickening of the senses to unaccustomed levels. As we moved forward, we expected at any second that the animal would explode into a furious announcement that he knew of our whereabouts. However, to our relief and feeling of anti-climax we found that it was dead and the flies were already laying eggs in the wound around the wire. The wire had started to shred from the animal's bites. The leopard had also bitten into his own leg in its fury and desperation to get away from the restraint and the pain of the wire that was cutting so remorselessly into its flesh.

We walked back to the Land Rover, strangely buoyant in the feeling of bravado that follows the facing of danger. I remember stopping in my tracks as a cobra wound its way across our path. Without saying a word, all three of us watched its black sinuous progress into the belukar. *I was happy that I had at least reached the stage where the appearance of a snake was now, for me, no longer unusual. I could take it in my stride just like the other people on the estate.*

I went back to the office, finished my work and gave instructions for the carcass of the leopard to be collected from the field. The Land Rover disappeared up the road to Sungai Lembing with a driver and a young pregnant Tamil woman, Munniamah, who was about to give birth. She was to be admitted to the maternity ward and her husband was sitting anxiously in the back of the vehicle on one of the side seats. I gave permission for the lorry to drive out to bring in the leopard. I watched the ancient Bedford climb the hill past my bungalow loaded down with curious young men, all anxious to get a closer look at the animal. I also gave instructions that the animal was not to be mutilated until we had decided what to do with it. From previous experience I knew that the whiskers, the claws, the teeth, the testicles and penis and even the eyes would be removed to make ubat. *'Ubat' is the Malay word*

*for medicine, or a cure, and the animal's parts would be looked
upon as medicine to strengthen a failing man's body, to bring the
strength of the animal into whoever ate the ubat. If you consumed a
soup made from the eyes, then your eyes would assume the strength
of vision of the leopard. His testicles would give you phenomenal
strength in bed and if you were to wear his whiskers as a talisman
you would be protected and saved from all fears.*

*I was drinking tea upstairs in the bungalow when I heard
the lorry come grinding its way up the back road and swing into
my driveway. I watched as 15 or so men jumped off the back of the
lorry to be met by my half-heartedly barking dogs. The dogs knew
these men. However, when the dogs got wind of the leopard they
flew back into the house barking with dedicated seriousness. The
leopard was carried up the steps and placed on the porch in front
of the main entrance. I walked down the stairs and turned into the
hall where the dogs were creating an enormous din. The boxer had
wet the floor with his urine. I continued past them out to the steps
where the leopard had been placed. The dogs gingerly followed me
but when we reached the leopard Barney crept forward to sniff, and
then both dogs broke speed records to get past me and out to the
open space of the lawn where they continued their terrified barking,
incapable of approaching the animal to see that it was dead.*

*I asked if anyone could arrange to skin the animal for me. A
surly, Tamil tapper, Vadiveloo, stepped forward and we agreed on a
price. I said I wanted some of the teeth and the claws and awarded
the rest equally to the watchman and Subramanium.*

*The animal must have died an indescribably painful and
unworthy death, and that death must have occurred at least a
couple of days before the three of us went up to look at it. The
meat would have been useless to eat, but if boiled into some sort
of slimy 'ubat', no doubt some of the men could be induced to pay*

something for a bowl full.

I delivered a lecture about the evils of setting snares and told everyone that I would have to inform the Game Department and that could mean we would soon be swarming with Game Rangers trying to find a culprit. Nobody was in favour of Game Rangers poking around, and I knew that by threatening everybody with the arrival of officious Rangers, looking for handouts and searching for all sorts of things such as an illegal liquor destillery would mean that my labourers would remain completely silent. No one in their right mind wants trouble with the authorities. I never did report the illegal trapping and death of the leopard. It would have been too much of a run-around with the Game Department, with forms to fill in and questions to answer, for nothing. The poor animal was already dead. All I could do was continue my battle against snares.

The pelt was inexpertly cured when I eventually received it from Vadiveloo, who had done the skinning. I made things worse by scraping away at uncured sections and rubbing salt into the whole pelt. For several mornings I placed the pelt, flesh side up, to further cure in the sun. The result was a shrunken thin hard board of leopard skin, almost unrecognisable as a leopard and a horrible travesty of the animal's original beauty. The pelt, which I sent to my nephew in England is, I think, now in the bottom of some cupboard or completely forgotten in the corner of a loft in Dorset.

CHAPTER 17

Back To Panching

There used to be a railway line stretching from Panching village following the road and heading out towards the Kuantan River. Along the railway line, the estate road dips down a hill leaving the railway and turns slightly north. The land on both sides of the road resembled old tin tailings, an open area with no trees and poor soil given over to a mixture of grasses, *lalang* and *belukar*. It was a good area for snipe and I would often see the birds on their long, knitting-needle legs skittering in and out from the protection of the grasses growing along the side of the road.

When latex collection from the North Division was completed, the weighing done and the crop-books entered, it would be about 1:30 pm. Leaving the *mandors* to wash the utensils and tidy up, I would walk back along that road and join the railway line in the direction of the factory. It was the hottest, most weary trip of the day. We were not aware in those days of the importance of fluids. I had perhaps walked and climbed hills on the Estate for three of four hours after breakfast without water. And I remember that particular walk back to the factory, as the time when I asked myself, what on earth I was doing there, in that sun-soaked and wild corner of Malaya? I would imagine my friends back in England being suddenly transposed to join me on this walk for a few minutes to see what it was really like, this exotic life in the tropics. The sun hammered down on the top of my head and shoulders and neck with a heat that built up with such intensity that if I put my hand up to touch my head I could feel the heat of my hair burn my scalp. I never wore a hat. I should have done, at least on those occasions when it was impossible to find shade and I just had to walk, or not get back at all.

When I lived at Panching and at Nada, I spent some time in Sungai Lembing. I played cricket, swam in the rather miserable concrete-lined swimming pool, visited the bungalows of bachelor friends, and, occasionally, I would be invited to the houses of more senior European couples for an evening meal. Friday was poker night in the European club. I played cards with Peter Mathias, a mining engineer from India, John Burn, an electrical engineer—who was, a few years later to become my best man when I got married—and several other bachelors. We drank beer at duty-free prices, and gambled with desperate concentration for relatively sensible limits. After an evening's fun we would take off for the village and visit Ah Lai to order a *mee*, a *mee hoon*, a fried *mee*, a *keoy teoh* or a *nasi goreng*. These meals were always eaten with chopsticks and with plenty of sliced or pickled chillies and a final glass of beer. I would then drive home to Nada, 10 or so miles along a totally isolated jungle and estate road in a semi-intoxicated state, or worse. Some mornings, when I woke up, I could remember nothing of the trip home. That scared me. On one of these trips when I was not inebriated, a tiger bounded across the road in front of me. I got out of the Land Rover in order to get that strong, unmistakable smell of musky cat.

I continued to visit Sungai Lembing after the move to Panching. It was a longer and more tortuous drive along the laterite roads through the newly planted southern part of Kuala Reman Estate. The road then narrowed to a stony track, twisting and dipping through undeveloped land abundant with high arching, elegant bamboos and magnificent jungle trees. There were many swamps and impenetrable mats of sedge grass and thicket, ideal for monitor lizards and wild pig. The road then climbed back up into humpy terrain through the whole of Nada, until it flattened out again in the Ampang fields. I was always relieved to arrive at the tarmac surface on the approach road down the hill into Sungai Lembing. The relief was in being able to drive on a smooth surface without having the teeth rattled out of my head by the potholes and gullies in the road.

One evening after a trip to the club in Sungai Lembing I arrived home, quite late, at the assistant's bungalow on the hill at Panching. The electricity supply to both the manager's and the assistant's bungalows was generated by a diesel engine situated at the rear of the manager's bungalow. There was no provision for electricity to the staff, to the shops, or to the labour force. They all had to supply their own light, usually an inexpensive and inadequate oil lamp or kerosene-operated pressure blinders with an incandescent mantle one should not stare into.

George Wood was much more of a man for staying up and reading than was Maurice Cotterill. Even so, my bungalow was in darkness when I pulled up at the entrance porch. The small kerosene lamp, set in place by my gardener, had a round, metal reflector with a picture of the Chinese film actress, Lin Dai, from Hong Kong. I came to be very fond of her even though I only had her face to look at. I was once told by a Chinese acquaintance, that it was said that Lin Dai was deemed to be so beautiful that men ejaculated by just looking at her. My particular Lin Dai was left burning just inside the door to the stairs leading up to the second floor of the bungalow.

I parked the Land Rover in the porch and checked to see that the dogs had water. I picked up the lamp and carefully walked upstairs, preceded by the leaping and dancing shadows cast by a single Lin Dai kerosene lamp.

I cleaned my teeth and washed in water scooped from a

Shanghai jar. On my way to the bathroom, I passed my bed ,where I noticed that the mosquito net had been lowered to the ground and was draped around the bed touching the wooden floor. I was pleased that the net was in place and that it would not then be necessary for me to reach up above the bed to the rectangular frame from which the net was draped. As I cleaned my teeth, I recalled that, with the poor light from my lamp, I had noticed that my brilliantly red pyjamas placed on the pillow, but I had also noticed the cord from the pyjama trousers stretched out across the bed. I knew it was the cord, as the colour from the pyjamas had run, and the cord was all shades of red and pink. I thought that was very strange. Why would Ah Moi have pulled out the cord? For a second I speculated that perhaps she had pulled it out during washing, and did not manage to get the cord back into the waistline.

I dismissed these thoughts and padded across the bungalow in bare feet. The last thing I always did before getting into bed was to walk out to the veranda and listen to the night. It was incredibly silent, with the generator engine turned off. If there was moonlight the bungalow *toc-toc* bird that always took up a position around my compound would be busy and perhaps, if I was lucky, I could hear the trumpeting sound of an elephant or the sawing pant of a tiger. In the distance away over the fields towards Kolek I could sometimes hear the occasional explosion of a Loosco elephant scarer. But that night all was quiet and I heard just the stirring of my own dogs seeking safety under the stairs, and the odd, plaintive yap of a disturbed dog in Panching village. Even at night I enjoyed the sight of Bukit Ceras, dark and menacing, looming above the fields and the flat country to the west.

I went back into the bedroom to get into my bed. Just before I blew the flame out of Lin Dai, I noticed that the pyjama cord had moved and one of the ends was raised searchingly off the sheet, sensing in my direction. It was a coral snake. They can be quite deadly, but they have a small mouth. Deaths from coral snakes were not as frequent as deaths from banded kraits or cobras.

Unfortunately, I had to kill it. Snakes had no business being in my bungalow and certainly not in my bed. To kill it, I used my walking stick, which was always close to hand. Draping the snake over the stick, I guessed it to be about three feet in length. I tossed it from the upstairs veranda into the garden. After carefully looking around the veranda, and the lounge, and the bedroom for brothers, or sisters, or mates, I got into bed. Meticulously, I tucked the mosquito net in, under the mattress all around the bed, making sure that every available inch of net was off the floor. I also took a battery-operated torch to bed with me and carefully swept the beam across the floor of the bedroom, an operation I repeated every two minutes or so. I remembered having heard that snakes often hunt or travel in pairs, and, if there is one snake there may well be two. Finally, before dropping off to sleep, I made a mental note to get the gardener to remove every creeping plant that festooned the walls of the old wooden bungalow. Exhausted, I eventually dropped off to sleep and dreamt of a seductive vision of Lin Dai covered in snakes, drifting around my room showing up only when caught in the beam of my torch.

The production of natural rubber

At the end of every month, each and every activity that took place on the estate had to be calculated and costed-out; that meant that the exact cost of each operation was recorded into a disbursement sheet called a distribution. For me, it was a nightmare. At that time, before computers and even before pocket calculators, young assistants on most rubber estates in the country toiled away for at least two or perhaps even for three nights, to complete the monthly accounts. Nights with little sleep, hunched over pocket check rolls, crop record books and EPF accounts, with only the glow from an insect-invaded oil lamp creating a tiny island of light in isolated bungalows surrounded by rubber trees and a sleeping Malaya.

The weighing-in books would record that Ramakrishnan had, for example, harvested 225 lbs, dry rubber content (DRC) at 18 cents per lb from his Charu task, and 146 lbs at 22 cents from his Ampang task. In addition, there had been one wash-out, he had received an advance of 30 ringgits and was a member of the EPF. All entries in the massive Big check roll itself, the definitive document, had to be made in my hand writing. It was no good to pay a kerani to do the check roll for me. Maurice Cotterill insisted that I made all the calculations and performed each and every addition or subtraction, as well as every other book-keeping entry, and God help me, if there were errors.

This arduous task involved developing my own system for computing the monthly wages for every person working on the estate. The most difficult to work out were the yields of the tappers. The drivers, factory workers, field labourers, contractors and chokras (children, employed for extra work—really a type of cheap labour, but a chance for some families to increase income), were much easier in comparison. They were either paid monthly, as was the case for drivers, or a fixed rate per day, multiplied by the number of days worked. These calculations were all done by hand on scrap paper. Calculators—the mechanically operated Facit with its crank handle and pinging bell were on the market, but beyond my pocket. The electronic devices we so casually use today were still not invented.

Tappers were often employed in two or three different areas of the estate. Yields, in terms of latex per tapping, varied in accordance with the clone, but at Nada the whole estate was planted with so-called unselected seedlings. Other influences on the trees that affected the yields were the age of the trees, soil conditions, drainage, ease of access, whether or not the tapper had a long carry to get to a reception shed; a hilly area difficult to climb, root disease such as fomes lignosus, which decimates the stand and reduces yield, the presence of mistletoe, and other factors that had an influence on the all important yield per acre.

At Nada, we were infested with a fungus disease called mouldy rot, which attacks and destroys the tapping panel. The greyish mould eats into the newly-tapped bark. Treatment is costly and demanding, and at times involves attempting to get the tapper to disinfect his knife between each tree. An anti-fungal preparation called Fomac was used for treatment. It contained a violet dye for ease of supervision, so that one could easily recognise the trees that had been treated. I used to think the treated trees looked like rows and rows of blowzy women with too much lipstick and twisted smiles.

Each tapper was allocated at least two different tasks at Nada because at that time it was an old stand of rubber and most tapping was on 100 per cent exploitation. That means that all trees planted on the estate with a circumference of more than 20 inches were tapped for half their circumference, every second day. A task consisted of the number of trees allocated to a tapper and actually tapped in a day's work varied between, 250 and 300 trees. The estate was divided into two halves to facilitate collection and supervision. All the tapping work was carried out in one half of the estate on one day and in the other half of the estate on the next day

Tapping involved an early start. It was a wonderful time of the day on the estate, and a bit frightening. Tappers often went to work with a carbide-operated light attached to their foreheads, carrying their buckets on a kanda stick across their shoulders. It was eerie to see them disappearing into the unending darkness of tunnels of rubber trees, occasionally flashing illumination into the canopies as they looked up at a startled owl or stepped aside for a massive spider's web. Calling out to each other for encouragement, the noises they made broadcast their presence to chase off a late-feeding pig or even a lurking tiger

The tapper pulls off and removes the strip of scrap rubber or the congealed latex left from the previous tapping. This, together with what is coagulated in the cup from late drip, is placed in a bag slung over the tapper's shoulder. The smell is foul. The protein constituents of the latex are rapidly sought out and attacked by bacteria, and the chemical changes give off foul sulphurous gases.

An old tree is difficult to tap as the tapping panel usually comprises of renewed bark that has been tapped at least once before. The nicks and wounds of previous tapping operations grow out into irregularities, or small lumps on the tapping panel. This means that when the tapper has to tap into renewed bark, he or she will have to make many carefully chosen cuts in order to avoid cutting too deep and nicking into the cambium of the tree and leading to even more wounding.

Supervision of the tappers was a job done by a mandor, a labouring supervisor in charge of perhaps 30 tappers. His job (I never met a female tapping mandor, although it could have been possible) was to ensure among other jobs that the tappers observed a code of cleanliness that involved keeping bark and sand and earth particles out of the cups and making sure that buckets were properly washed. This was very important, as dirty utensils meant that the bacteria I mentioned earlier also lead to a process starting in freshly collected latex called pre-coagulation. This results in lumpy latex before it even gets to the processing factory. If this happens, it cuts down the yield, clogs up the metal filters when the latex is poured *into the tanks at the factory and, most importantly, leads to a reduction in the quality of the rubber produced. If pre-coagulation is a major problem on an estate, in spite of efforts at cleanliness, the tappers are issued with an anti-coagulant solution and the same solution is added to the field collection tanks transported by lorry or tractor. A latex anti-coagulant is a material that is added to latex in order to prevent coagulation by natural means before the latex reaches the factory for processing. Anti-coagulants are particularly useful in wet weather and with the lattices of certain clones that have a tendency to pre-coagulate. For the preparation of sheet rubber, sodium sulphite, ammonia or formalin can be used as anticoagulants. The use of these solutions increases the cost of production, and dosage is critical in terms of mixing the correct concentration and the quantities used. Using anticoagulants in the field and in the collection tanks leads to increased requirements of*

Sungai Talam Estate, 1958. Cyclone damage to a stand of four-year-old trees.

formic acid in the aluminium coagulating tanks in the factory.

The mandor *also made sure that the tappers maintain the side channels, which are required on each tree. Every individual tapped tree that is exploited on a 100 per cent tapping system is tapped or cut into by only a half of its circumference. This is carefully measured, and a light cut in the bark is made by drawing the tapping knife vertically down the tree on both sides. It is easy to measure if a tapper exceeds the half circumference of the tree. At the same time, by using a bark tester the mandor can also check to make sure that the full half-circumference of bark is correctly utililised. A tapping knife has a steel, curved blade and the part of the blade furthest from the handle is flattened out and bent to an angle of slightly more than 90 degrees. The knife is more of a double-sided gouge and it is kept razor sharp at the front, for pushing, and at the inside of the curve for pulling. If a tapper taps too deep into the tree, he wounds the tapping panel by cutting into the cambium and this triggers a growth response from the surrounding cells in order to protect the tree. If a tapper is too light-handed and taps too shallow, then he or she does not open or slice into all the available latex vessels, and yields suffer.*

Finally, the mandor *supervises monthly bark consumption and ensures that the coal-tar spots, or paint spots (called spot marks) are marked on the panel on the last day of each month. He also checks to make sure that the placing of the galvanised tin spouts is in the optimum position, and that the cup is correctly replaced in the wire cup-holder between tappings to collect after-drip, and not just left on the ground to pick up soil particles. On the old trees at Nada, with fifteen tappings a month in good weather, we allowed only one inch of bark consumption. Working on the premise that bark is the estate's capital asset, it is apparent that one must not tap, or cut away more bark than absolutely necessary. In theory, a*

Sungai Talam Estate, 1957. Chinese female tapper Hoo Way Fong, returning from her task with two buckets of latex in Field 13.

razor-thin sliver of bark cut along the length of the tapping panel is sufficient to open up the latex vessels and allow the latex to flow along the cut, down to the metal spout and into the cup.

The best time to start tapping is in the very early morning, before dawn, to take advantage of the miracle of transpiration or the upward flow of water and nutrients from the roots of the tree to the upper branches and leaves. As the day wears on and the ambient heat increases the millions of stomata on the underside of the leaves of the tree close down to prevent excessive moisture loss. The upward flow of latex then slows down and stops altogether at about 10:30–11:00 am. The ultimate time for collection is to arrive at each tree exactly when the flow has stopped and the residue of latex on the tapping cut is at the early stage of coagulating, to naturally seal off the cut.

A tree is tapped from left to right. In old rubber the angle is about 30 degrees. The reason for this is that the latex vessels in the bark are inclined at an angle of three-and-a-half degrees to the right.

Therefore, a cut from high-left to low-right (with the observer facing the tree) slices through a greater number of latex vessels per unit length of tapping cut, as compared to a high-right to low-left cut. Trials have shown that yields of left-to-right, as compared to right-to-left tapping are greater by about ten per cent. I am sorry to say there were a great number of planters in Malaya who could not answer, if asked why we tapped from left to right—the usual reply being that most tappers are right-handed, and it is more natural to approach the tree from left to right. I only came by this knowledge by reading Mr A.T. Edgar's bible for all rubber planters, Manual of Rubber Planting (Malaya) 1960*—a fantastic reference and guide. This book helped me enormously when studying for the Associate Diploma examinations conducted by The Incorporated Society of Planters, Technical Education Scheme. I am immensely proud to add the letters AISP after my name.*

CHAPTER 18

Ah Moi

This is a chapter about about Ah Moi. And it is about me. In so many ways it would be easier, more expedient to just put her behind me, like a passed-over episode of my life. But that would not be fair. In fact, to ignore her as part of my life in Malaya during those first four years would be totally unjust to her and small-minded of me. The difficulty I face is how to present her in the correct light; how to convey her fundamental kindness, honesty and innocence, while preserving some honour at the same time. Just expressing these thoughts is a stupid attempt at laying down the rules in order to cope with the telling of her story. Another reason for telling this story is that we had an indelible effect on each other's lives. In a sense it was an irreplaceable love, built on youth, desperation and circumstances that can never return, and in so many ways, it ruined her life, at least in accordance with the Chinese standards that existed in Malaya fifty years ago.

It was unthinkable for a Chinese girl to enter into an intimate relationship with a man before marriage. In those days in Europe and Asia, purity was the prize taken by a girl into her union. It was the key to making a good match, a match in which Chinese pragmatism and wisdom anticipated a successful continuation of the family and the well-being of the elderly. Innocence was necessary to make a good marriage.

At that time, for all Asian girls living in Malaya, that is girls in the Malay, Chinese or Indian communities, if they were not virgins, then they were considered to be 'used goods', an object of shame to their parents. The girl therefore would not be able to procure a sound marriage with an eligible man. It was doubly unthinkable and horrifying for a decent Chinese girl to enter into a relationship with a European. For the traditional Chinese living in Malaya two generations ago, the very thought of having a daughter who consorted in an intimate way with an Englishman would be anathema. Exactly in the same way that a European would have been despised in most expatriate circles if he consorted openly with an Asian girl.

In recalling and balancing the elements of Ah Moi's story with the truth, the story is not kind to me. In all our lives, there are times when we search for mitigating factors; we pursue lines of thought that may excuse and explain unkindness when discovered in us.

The snow is fiddling at the windows on this dark Norwegian morning. The wind has ruffled the waters of the fjord sufficiently to break up the early skin of ice that yesterday was forming in the sheltered bays and inlets. It is difficult to think back over almost 50 years.

We first met at Sungai Talam. She was working for Brian Gahan together with another Chinese girl in the bungalow; they were both employed to do the cleaning, cooking and washing. It is a bit preposterous to refer to them as girls; Ah Moi was about twenty-seven and her companion, Ah Kum, a couple of years older. They had both been rubber tappers, and both had the characteristic dark facial complexion of Chinese labourers used to working all day under the Malayan sun. George Wood and I agreed to employ both women, and after four months, when George left Sungai Talam and I was to live alone in the bungalow, I could not afford to employ them both. Ah Moi chose to stay. My Malay was poor and she said to me through Mr Thomas who served as an interpreter:

"I am unable to cook European meals, except for basic dishes like bacon and egg and stews. I can boil potatoes. Please do not get angry with me if I am unable to prepare the food you want."

"Of course not," I replied, and assured her that I was easy-going when it came to food. I tried to continue in Malay and said, "Ah Moi, *saya suka makanan orang China. Kalau* Ah Moi *boleh masak makanan China, bagus!* Ah Moi, I like Chinese food. If you will cook Chinese food for me, that will be very good."

She smiled and continued to look at me, uncertain, hesitating—waiting for me to say more. "I would like you to work for me." I said, lamely, also feeling uncertain as to how the whole relationship would work out. It was finally agreed that she would continue and live in the servant's quarters at the bungalow. And I suppose that was the time when, inevitably, the paths of our lives joined in a weird employer-servant, *tuan-amah*, man–woman intimacy.

It was about 8:00 am one bright sunny morning, when the mist had cleared the canopy of the trees and the heat of the sun was pushing through and burning up the ground. Ah Moi and Ah Kum cycled towards me on their way back to the bungalow after having been in Kuantan for a day off. Ah Moi's hair was free of the usual elastic bands, and it framed her face in brilliant black waves. She was wearing a tight-fitting *sam foo*, and she was slim and lovely. She smiled so warmly and shyly called out, "*Selamat pagi*," as she cycled past.

It started in abject loneliness. We were both lonely. I used to invite her in the evening to come and sit in the lounge, and she would bring her Chinese comics and magazines. I did not touch alcohol in those early days and we would share a bottle of soft drink. We would read or listen to the radio. She helped me to learn Malay. I pointed to objects and said the word in English, she repeated the English word and then told me the Malay word.

"Chair," I would point.

"Chair," she responded. "*Kerusi, ker-us-i.*" I copied her way of saying things, and noted the words down in my notebook.

I should write Ah Moi's story. But each time I face up to the task of searching into that part of the past, I meet the pain that I caused her and then I am ashamed. It is like a roadblock. The easiest action is to turn round and walk away. That is why I continue to put the task from me.

Snakes behind my head

On certain afternoons I left the divisional office at Nada and worked in the bungalow office. At agreed times, I would crank the telephone in order to relay information about yields and other facts and figures to the office at Panching. It was a landline telephone and the telephone posts and the wire belonged to the Pahang Consolidated Company Limited at Sungai Lembing. The two divisions of the estate were coupled up to the tin mine's system of telecommunications and, from each division, we could also contact the telephone exchange at Sungai Lembing. One ring was to the mineshaft at Sungai Rimau, two rings were for Panching, three rings for the Sungai Lembing exchange and four rings for the Nada bungalow. The phone was a hand-crank affair and each ring was a rapid circular movement of the wrist. The telephone was situated downstairs in my bungalow in the assistant's own private offic,e where the old iron safe with a massive brass handle was used to deposit cash and the cartridges for the estate shotgun.

It was breathlessly hot that afternoon, without a suggestion of a breeze, and I leant back in my chair, resting my head against a blackboard that was nailed up on two hooks behind my head. The blackboard was used to chalk up tapping schedules, important dates such as when the doctor or the Labour Officer were due to visit. I had the telephone in my left hand and I was listening to the crackles on the line and the distant head office noises. I had made the connection to Panching and I was waiting to speak to Mr Cherian, the Chief Clerk.

In the heat of the afternoon, my prayers were answered and a warm breeze gently ruffled the papers on my desk. Gazing out of the open shutters at the tops of the rubber trees in Field 4 I became aware of a scratching sound behind my head. At first I thought it was a kumbang, a large beetle, or perhaps a striped hornet building a nest with dabs of mud behind the board. But then I felt a movement; a vibration that rippled through the blackboard and into the back of my head; a powerful and unmistakeable feeling that something of substance was behind my head. It made me jump out of my seat. I swung round and stared hard at the board and the wall. Suddenly a black tail, about a foot long slipped out from under the board. It was far too big to be the tail of a rat. At first I thought it might be a large lizard, which had climbed the wall and lodged itself behind the blackboard, hunting insects.

I fetched my walking stick, and, stretching out to arms-length, I eased the blackboard away from the wall. Intertwined and writhing quite vigorously were two copulating black cobras. They were caught up between the blackboard and the uneven planks behind. In a few seconds they both slipped to the cement floor. They uncoupled and immediately assumed attack position, hissing and swaying together in remarkable unison.

I stepped back out of distance in case they should spit, and watched them staring at me. They were swaying slightly from side to side continuing to move in unison. Resolutely it seemed, and at exactly the same time, they turned half away from me, keeping me in their side vision, and surprisingly quickly they snaked across the *floor of the office, under the skirting board, across the cemented five-foot-way and the drain, and out over the lawn to disappear in the rubber. Their movements were identical, except that one of them kept about two feet in front of the other snake. I guessed it was the male keeping its head higher than its partner's. But what struck me, as they moved across the floor and over the grass, was that they moved perfectly together in a harmony of communication and movement that convinced me that they instinctively assumed the best defensive position, and that was to move as if they were one larger creature with two heads.*

CHAPTER 19

Sungai Lembing Cut Off By Floods

During the monsoon at the end of 1959, the rains were so severe and sudden that flash floods occurred wreaking enormous damage to property and causing some loss of life. The road and the railway link to Sungai Lembing were washed away. The road washed out at a point where a gulley was channeled under the road in a large culvert pipe. It was at a point where one of the steep, *lalang*-covered hills that hem in the mine and the village made it necessary to construct the road out on the shoulder of the hill. There was a sheer drop down to the river on the outside of the road. The force of water had overflowed the culvert and eroded the rocks and soil packed around the pipes beneath the tarmac. Eventually, a whole section of road was swept away into the river a hundred feet below. The soil and the weight of water slid down the hillside to engulf the railway line. Several yards of the line were also carried away leaving parallel lengths of metal suspended in mid-air, still attached to the wooden sleepers, useless like a child's section of twisted model rail.

The telephone lines were out. I drove in a Land Rover, with rain pouring down in grey sheets of water, to explore the damage to our own property and our own bridges. Much of the plantation was inundated, and I could only check so far in certain directions to see that the drains and streams were coping with the enormous amounts of water. When I reached the estate boundary to the west, I carried on up towards Sungai Lembing to see if I could find where the telephone line was broken. I parked the Land Rover just off the road at the junction to Sungai Remau. I instructed

Major, the boxer dog to stay in the Land Rover. In his half-blind way, he stared unhappily back at me. It would have been useless telling Barney to do likewise. He trotted after me and we climbed the hill to skirt the landslide where the road had been. Looking down through the cleft, where the volume of water had breached the whole road trace, there was a frightening drop and I realised there was little in the way of shrubs or trees to hold on to if I started to slide.

After half an hour of walking, I arrived in the village of Sungai Lembing where everything was in a bad state of flood. I met Henry Hodding, who was Number Two or Deputy general manager at the mine. He was trying to get around the village in an Austin car in order to survey the damage. I gave him the news of what I had seen of damage on my walk to the mining community. Henry shook his head sadly, "Bloody nuisance, this. For the first time for years we were going to turn in some reasonable financial results, and then all this damage occurs." Snapping out of his despondency, he smiled and invited me for breakfast. By this time, my dog, Barney, was nowhere to be seen. I had noticed that he had been showing some interest in a local female dog that seemed quite keen to meet a new male from the jungle. I decided to leave him for the time being and pick him up later.

"The whole road is out completely," I told Henry. "And the section of road that has gone seems to have avalanched down the hillside, and it has taken out the railway line."

"We have driven up to have a look at it," said Henry. "If this rain continues it will take us a few days to repair, but I have ordered stone from the mill so we can start filling the railway gap with something more substantial than top soil." He slowed down and changed gear and then revved the engine to get through a section of road that was badly flooded. "The road won't be so easy," he continued. "The land below the road will need some sort of shoring up, and we will have to cut into the side of the hill and make a new trace."

When we reached Henry's bungalow, up on the side of the hill overlooking the village, he offered me a change of clothing, and breakfast, which I gratefully accepted, as I was wet through like a freshly emerged water rat. His wife, Anne joined us. She was looking pretty and feminine in what was for me a surprisingly disconcerting experience. It had been some time since I had been in the company of a youngish and attractive European woman. She looked radiant with pale skin and carefully applied make-up.

"How are things on the estate?" she asked.

"Well, our North Division is inaccessible, so we do not know how things are over there, but everything else is fine except some of the low-lying areas are under water. The Ampang *kongsi* houses are flooded, but we have a rowing boat down there to ferry people with young kids."

"Pasir Kemudi is flooded, and the Charu River and I expect Batu Sawah will be impassable," said Henry. "So here we are, stuck."

"What's new?" demanded Anne, staring at Henry with the look of indifference a wife reserves for her husband.

"I was supposed to go to Kuala Lumpur," she continued, facing me with a smile. "We don't have a damn phone as all the wires are down, so I can't even get a message to the hotel." She shook her long blond hair in a gesture of irritation. "I am supposed to be meeting friends. They are passing through from Australia." She lit a cigarette. "They are making the stopover in KL especially for me." She thrust her crossed legs out in front of her and leaned back in her chair, the thin material of her white and blue dress falling away to the floor. She was the picture of a woman used to getting her own way.

"Well, we can't control the weather my dear," Henry said, an attempt at levity in his voice. Anne ignored him.

"I can't even play tennis in this," she gestured disdainfully outside at the continuing downpour.

When we had had our breakfast, I was dropped off at the point where I had left Barney and started searching for him. I followed the river and looked for any pack of dogs pursuing an interloper. He was nowhere to be found. And, he, of course, did not even know that I had been picked up in a car and whisked away for an hour or two. Speaking Malay, and working on the assumption that local people notice most things that are out of the ordinary, I asked several locals if they had seen a strange dog. Malays have a fear of dogs because a dog's snout is considered to be unclean. The Malays I asked would perhaps only have noticed a strange dog in order to avoid it. Some Chinese eat dogs, so the Chinese men I asked probably would have only paid as much attention to a dog that crossed their path as Europeans would notice a village chicken.

When Henry came back to pick me up in his car there was still no sign of Barney. I had been offered a trip by rail through the mine, travelling straight through the mountain to the other side at Sungai Remau, almost to the point where I had left my Land Rover. This trip would save me a great deal of walking in the rain. I felt heartless about abandoning my dog, but I had work to do and resolved to find him later.

We shuddered and hurtled from side to side, the intense darkness of the mine pulled by a small-gauge diesel locomotive. I was shocked and amazed at just how tiny the tunnels were. It was imperative to keep arms and hands inside the wagon as fingers could easily have been crushed or an arm torn off in the crazy rocking movement of the train. The trip took about ten minutes and I thought to myself that there was no possibility of my dog following my trail. I had been transported by car to the mine head, and then by rail through the mountain, and all the time the rain was falling in buckets enough to wash away any trace of my smell. Barney was on his own, in a strange, flooded village about eight miles away from his home.

When I reached the Land Rover, Major was still in position sitting in the back of the vehicle under the canvas hood hunched up against the driving rain. He stared suspiciously and unseeingly out at my approaching form. From some distance away I could see him push his snout out in front of him, desperately trying to pick up scents of recognition from the impossibly wet air. He exploded into wild shakings and snorting in great joy at my return. I had half-hoped that Barney would have made it back to the vehicle when he discovered that I was no longer around the spot where he had left me in the village, but he was not there.

I drove home with Major and carried on with the duties of the day in total isolation from Panching because the Sungai Charu was flowing in rapid torrents over the top of the bridge. We continued sorting the final stock of rubber and grading the ribbed smoked sheet into bales of 248.89 lbs, almost exactly nine bales to the ton. Because of so many days without any tapping activity, we had not processed any rubber in the factory. The accumulated stock in the packing shed had all been sorted and packed into bales in preparation for shipping. The almost empty smokehouse was prepared for a thorough clean-up. The only advantage of having days of uninterrupted rain was that stock-taking was now possible with the utmost accuracy. As the day progressed, the rain eased and eventually by the evening there were some brief glimpses of sunshine that made the world steam.

I had my tea in the bungalow at Nada and once more set out in the Land Rover on the journey back to Sungai Remau, from where I was prepared to walk back up to Sungai Lembing in search of my dog. I left Major at home; with his poor eyesight and without Barney to act as his eyes, he could well be more of a hindrance than a help. The thought also crossed my mind that wildlife, disturbed by the constant rain and the flooding, could, in the search for food, be tempted to venture closer to the estate and the roads. I desperately hoped that Barney would not meet a leopard or a tiger if he were on the way back home.

I drove past the estate boundary at a point where the road dips down and curves again back up a hill affording a good view of the road. To my surprise and joy I caught sight of something black, an animal. It had paused to take in the sound of the Land Rover. It was Barney at the top of the rise, now determinedly trotting along the road, tongue lolling, but moving forward towards the sound of the engine and coming in my direction. He gave me a couple of wags of his tail, and without further ado, trotted round to the rear of the vehicle and jumped up into the back of the Land Rover.

I estimate that if he had followed the road trace, Barney had travelled about ten miles along a road he had only experienced from the back of the Land Rover. I turned the vehicle round and Barney shoved himself into his usual position, supporting himself between my shoulder and the top of the spare wheel that was bolted to the back of the seat. I could feel he was tired and pleased to be back because he put a lot of weight on me and he licked my neck and cheek a couple of times.

We drove home to the bungalow and Barney jumped down from the vehicle as soon as I parked in the porch-way. Major was also overjoyed and wagged his whole body, but was quickly dissuaded from too much familiarity and put in his place by a fierce throat growl from the top dog.

After a quick urinating trip at favourite spots in the garden, Barney trotted straight to the back of the bungalow, where he flopped down close to where Ah Moi was working. She too was pleased to see him, and she spoke to him in Cantonese in that special way she had, nodding her head at him, as if answering for him. It was earlier than his usual time but she gave him his metal dish filled with rice and food leftover from our table. When he had eaten, I called him over, brushed him and checked for ticks. He tried to settle to sleep, but his legs were still going and trembling, and he found it easier to stand and just pant, before flopping down again for another try.

CHAPTER 20

Monkey Attack

Barney hated monkeys. When he lived with me as my only dog on Sungai Talam Estate, I spent a weekend away, and that was the time he had chased monkeys on the edge of a replant, close to the jungle in Field 13. According to Mr Sidek he had managed to attack a baby monkey that had somehow had become separated from its mother.

"Your dog just followed me to the field, Sir. I did not call him. He was looking for you in the office early Saturday morning and he just followed me on my bicycle." Sidek was concerned that I would perhaps be angry. I could see the signs of nervousness in his boyish, round face. "Barney attacked a baby *monyet*. The monkey screams were terrible. And then, all the monkeys came down from the trees, and *ooh, ooh, ooh,* they attacked. Big fellows, males, three, four," he signalled with the fingers of both hands. "They came running on the ground, jumping on him, on the dog, whoosh, two, three at a time. Jumping in and biting and pulling and all the other monkeys, young ones and old ones all making a terrible screaming." Sidek looked worried. His brow was sweating and he used his forefinger to wipe and shake it clear.

"Didn't anybody help?" I demanded. "No, not possible, too fast to do anything." Sidek shook his head. "But Barney, he gets away, he run back to me. Barney run back to me, and the monkeys run away back up in the trees. And then they run away to the *hutan*."

"This was out in Field 13?"

"Yes, Sir," he replied. "Vadiveloo was there with the lorry and we took him back to the office and Vadiveloo and I look at him and clean him. Then Vadiveloo drive him to Kuantan, to the Veterinary Surgeon. I think he must surely die."

"Thank you Mr Sidek. Thank you for doing that and looking after him. I know that Malays do not like dogs, so I am particularly grateful to you. Thank you again." I shook his hand. Later, Mr Sidek discretely received a carton of cigarettes.

I went off in search of Vadiveloo to similarly thank him.

Barney was tied up at the bungalow, feeling sore and very sorry for himself. But if he were not tied up, he would have tried to hobble down the road after me. His back was badly bitten, as was the case his jowls, ears and all four of his legs. I treated him with a solution the Indian vet had given me and it helped to prevent the flies from getting at his wounds and laying eggs. The vet had stitched him up with forty-five stitches and given him a massive shot of penicillin.

Monkey in the toolbox

After my dog Barney was attacked at Sungai Talam, he became paranoid as far as monkeys were concerned. Each time we went into the field, he was much less nonchalant than he used to be, and he showed much more distrust. If we were in 'monkey country', he would cock his head over to one side in order to pick up monkey signals. If we surprised a pack during a field trip Barney would go beserk, but in a very much more cautious way than the Barney of old. Instead of tearing after them he had become very circumspect and careful. If monkeys were put to flight across open land covered in belukar *and tall* lalang *or grass, he would pursue them by chasing after them through the grass, stopping up frequently to bounce high up in the air, his head and shoulders clearing the undergrowth and standing on his two hind legs for a second or so, like a desert rat so he could catch sight of them or the movement of the grass.*

One morning, he surprised a pack alongside a jungle strip down at the Charu River. I had my walking stick, and Barney had been hanging back, investigating some tracks. He caught up just as the monkeys became aware of our presence, and, startled, they exploded into racing along the ground and leaping up into the lower branches of the trees. Screeching and chattering, they climbed high to the topmost branches and then launched themselves out across the river, leaping out and down and clutching the branches of the trees on the opposite bank.

Suddenly, a baby monkey, which must have lost its grip on its mother's back, fell off from its mother and plunged straight into the river. Before Barney realised what had happened, I jumped into the shallow water. The baby was tiny, and it was stunned, shocked and screaming under the water. I grabbed it quite hard behind its head, so that it could not bite me, and took it back to the Land Rover where I quickly thrust it inside the toolbox under the driver's seat and slammed the lid.

The monkeys, now on the other side of the river, big brown and grey kraa, were furious. The males were hanging back spying at me, heads bobbing to and fro to see what was to be done. Under appropriate circumstances, they would have attacked, but there was too much of the human around me; too much man in the form of a Land Rover and all its smells, and I had a dog with me, and there was a walking stick that looked suspiciously like a gun. They would judge the chances of winning this battle as too small. They surmised that there was a real chance that they would have to sacrifice some of their numbers if they came after me. Accepting the odds, they stayed high in the trees on the other side of the river watching me carry off their baby, held in front of me with both hands as I knew that given the chance it would bite me in pure desperation to survive.

Barney jumped up into the rear of the Land Rover and we drove home. We employed a wash amah, Ah Thai, and her little daughter to help me to remove the leeches from my boots. I had a shower, or rather, I scooped water over myself from the Shanghai jar, then changed into *a clean shirt and shorts for breakfast. After breakfast, we had a look at the monkey; a male, tiny and petrified. Strangely, the dogs made no savage approaches and Barney, after a sniff or two, was no longer interested in the tiny creature. Ah Moi, Suppramanium the gardener, Ah Thai and her daughter all decided that it was best for the poor animal if it was taken back to the field.*

The dogs were tied and stayed behind at the bungalow where Ah Moi fed them Jacob's Cream Crackers in order to take their minds off the departing Land Rover. Driving back down the hill to the Charu, it was now the hottest part of the day; the sun, white and without mercy, crackled the hair. It was coming up to mid-day, and the monkeys had moved well into the shade of the jungle trees where they were resting. They were almost impossible to see, but the odd call of alarm could be heard as they picked up scents, or the tremble of something approaching. When I reached the spot where the baby monkey had fallen into the river I carried it across to the opposite bank. Stopping a few yards up the bank, the baby monkey was encouraged onto a tree branch, where, slowly and unsteadily, it climbed higher up into the leafy top branches. Ponderously and awkwardly, because of its young age, it turned its pathetically small head to look up, and then it turned back to look down at me with enormous dark, shiny eyes.

Returning to the other side of the river, I backed away to listen and watch. There were a few movements in the jungle trees and some tentative monkey sounds floated from the edge of the jungle towards me in the heat. The river rippled on over sand and stone, the bright reflected light sliced occasionally by the knife-like wings of a brilliant blue dragonfly. Looking back from the Land Rover I could make out careful activity around the trees near the river. Perhaps, in time, his mother would come and claim him. There are accounts, stories told by Malays, who say that when a baby monkey has the smell of human on it, it will be rejected, or worse, torn apart, even by its own mother.

CHAPTER 21

Going Home

One evening, when all the staff in the Panching office were busy looking at their watches in the fond hope that we could call an end to the day, I was called into the manager's office by George Wood. None of the office staff, including myself as the assistant manager, ever left the office until after the manager decided to call it a day. When Cotterill was manager, he just walked out without even a cursory goodnight flung over his shoulder. We knew he had gone when the office peon ran silently in through the door with a smile from ear to ear. We used to then stand at the door of the office and watch him disappear up through the young rubber in the direction of the Manager's bungalow to make sure he had actually left for the day. Towards the end of the afternoon, the peon was always in position sitting on a bench outside the manager's window in order to spring to his feet when the manager left and to bring the happy news that the *tuan* had gone home, and we were now free to leave. With George Wood it was different. He arrived at the office at 3:30 or 4:00 pm, and then worked sometimes until 6:00 pm, which was terribly unfair on the office staff who, should have ended the day at 5:00 pm.

"Sit down, Michael," said George, waving me into the wooden chair on the opposite side of his desk. The shutters were open on the northern side of the office and I could just see part of Bukit Cheras blocking the rest of the view. "I've had a letter from London," George continued importantly. We were all most attentive to letters from London. "You see we have been discussing the business of home leave. Officially, you have three months to go before you are due for home leave." He looked across the top of the desk and took a cigarette from his ever-present tin of 50 Players. He lit his own cigarette and then, as if suddenly remembering my presence, offered me a cigarette. I took one and lit it with my own lighter.

"Thank you George," I said for the cigarette. "That's correct. I have only done three years and nine months of my four-year contract." It was as if I wanted to give the impression that I wanted to serve out the remaining three months of my contract-time at all costs. The thought of going on leave before time, when I was so unprepared for the news was stupendously mind shaking, so incredibly impossible, even though from what he had said so far, I had only the merest glimpse of the possibility of home leave and, here, already, I was almost trembling with excitement.

It was all I could do to smoke my cigarette in what I desperately hoped would look like a composed man, a man under control, a man in charge of himself.

"I have recommended to London that you be sent home on leave early." George was studying me carefully to see if he could achieve some emotional advantage from the effect this news would have on me. We had never really discussed the question of whether or not I would renew my contract. Although I had never given the impression that George was my favourite man to work with, I had never indicated that I was against coming back to Kuala Reman after my six months' leave.

"Do they indicate terms, salary and period of second tour, how much leave at the end of it?" I tried to be calm. I tried to remember all the times this conversation had been rehearsed in my head on those interminably, desperate evenings, drinking tea and gazing out of the bungalow at the sunset, my eyes forlornly seeking solace in the vague direction of London.

George assumed his irritatingly superior, managerial tone, and began: "London have empowered me to offer you a three- year contract at the expiration of your six months' leave and that is to be followed by a six-month paid home leave period." He paused to close the file in front of him, as if he was concerned that I might snatch a glimpse of the letter from London. "You will be allowed to proceed home immediately on fully paid home leave for a full period of six months," and he hesitated, "with an increment in pay Michael, with an increment! What do think about it." His face broke out into an unaccustomed broad smile. I did not have the heart to point out that the increment was due to me in any event upon the completion of my four years, in other words in exactly three months' time.

I could not believe it. It was impossible to think that within just a few days I would be on the way back to England. But there would be so much to arrange. I would have to explain the situation to Ah Moi, others would have to be informed, my dogs would have to be cared for, bills paid, my personal belongings packed and put into storage. My God, it was November, would I get out before the monsoon cut off the roads by flooding the bridges. How would I travel? What clothes would I wear? I would be home for Christmas!

I naturally assumed that I would be able to stay with my mother and father. The thought that perhaps my staying with them for six months would be inconvenient never entered my head. But I was going home.

When the practical details were taken care of, I paid Ah Moi six months' leave-pay, and, fortunately, she agreed to look after my dog Barney and return to her father's house at Kampong Tanah Puteh, just outside Kuantan. George kindly agreed to look after Major, the half-blind boxer. When the time finally came for me to actually leave the estate and start my journey he also drove me to the airport at Batu Sembilan.

As the rubber trees around Panching slid past the window of the Land Rover, and I had my suitcase in the back with George's driver, I could still not believe this moment had come. It was like some precious dream, an experience we fantasise upon but push out of our mind as one of those unachievable golden moments in life, like passing an exam or suddenly achieving won... me.

George and I shook hands at the airport and he left to go back to the Kuantan Club. I climbed up the steps of the ancient DC3 and we took off, bound for Kuala Lumpur and the old airport in the centre of the city. As we climbed and turned northwards, I could see Bukit Cheras far out ahead of the aircraft, so small and so permanent, like a sentinel over the rows and rows of rubber trees that had been my life for almost four years. The aircraft continued to turn and headed west up into the clouds.

Home leave, reunion with my parents and family, meeting friends, trying to pick up again on an English way of life, trying to convey to those who were interested, what life was actually like on an estate in Malaya—all this was wonderful and at the same time tryingly difficult. To chop out almost four years of life and be transported to another world is an insupportable burden and an immeasurable gift. My life had changed, and in some ways the lives of my family and friends in England had stood still. When I accepted the job at that interview in London some four years earlier I felt that I was like a steel ball in a pinball machine. When the spring-loaded plunger was released, I was hurled along the markers of life to be deflected irreversibly away from the original course, but scoring points and lighting lights.

A Poem For Ah Moi

Whenever I wash rice in order to remove the hollow shells of insects
and the grit of the paddy field
And the powdery white milky starch that makes it sticky floats off
with a grain or two
I lean my weight on one leg and look down into
the cloudy cold water
And think of you.
As my fingers separate the hard jasmine scented grains
I see you in my mind's eye swirling in the milk.
You too are washing rice
Squatting on the cement by the cracked monsoon drain
At the back of the bungalow
And I know you are aware of my attentive look
My desire carried to you on the heat of a languid afternoon.

I see the taut cotton material of your sam foo
stretched tight over your slim thighs
Your heels close up to your buttocks, your back
bent over the saucepan of rice
Beras until boiled to nasi.
I mark the sweat of the afternoon heat making small damp patches
under your arms
And I know you smell clean and of cooking and wood
smoke and Chinese talc.

*And I watch you bring your forearm up to wipe away the sweat that
has run down your face and trembles at your chin.
I wanted you then with the intensity of youth
In my loneliness, and the hurt, and the uncertainty
of being so far from home.*

*Your feet in wooden clogs with the flowery plastic straps
Your hair reaching down your back restrained by a rubber band,
tight into the head.
And, when you poured off the starchy whiteness,
the colour of frothy thin milk
You were careful not to lose one single grain.
I dwell for a few seconds looking down into this rice
And, when I pour away that cloudy whiteness I am careful not
to lose a single grain.
And I think across the years, across the chasm of time
and circumstances
Of your hurt, and I ache to know how you are today,
how you are now.*

MICHAEL THORP
Sandvigen, Norway.